Helen just turned thirty. She w milestone. She's been a bit qui

Normally, however, she is a

She contributes to various publica

the *Sydney Morning Herald*

She is currently working on two projects ... the first is a novel tentatively titled *Fat* and the second is an anxiety and depression management book derived from bitter experience!

She is considering the purchase of a Doberman and lives in inner Sydney with a bloke.

Also by Helen Razer

Three Beers and a Chinese Meal, with Mikey Robins
In Pursuit of Hygiene

EVERYTHING'S
FINE
HELEN
RAZER

a beginner's guide to thwarting primary nihilism

𝒱

VINTAGE

A Vintage Book
published by
Random House Australia Pty Ltd
20 Alfred Street, Milsons Point, NSW 2061
http://www.randomhouse.com.au

Sydney New York Toronto
London Auckland Johannesburg
and agencies throughout the world

First published 1998
Copyright © Helen Razer 1998

National Library of Australia
Cataloguing-in-Publication Data

Razer, Helen.
Everything's fine : a beginner's guide to thwarting primary
nihilism.

ISBN 0 091 83925 4.

1. Australian wit and humour. I. Title.

A828.302

Design by Yolande Gray
Typeset by Asset Typesetting Pty Ltd, Sydney
Printed by Griffin Press, Netley, South Australia

10 9 8 7 6 5 4 3 2 1

EVERYTHING'S
FINE

CONTENTS

This book is dedicated to the memory of Molly Dog,
beloved Spaniel and companion for ten years

EVERYTHING'S
FINE
ACKNOWLEDGEMENTS

EMPATHIC FOLK: THIS BOOK WAS KNOCKED INTO SHAPE AT A TIME OF CONSIDERABLE PERSONAL DISTRESS. I WOULD BE A TOTAL NUT JOB WERE IT NOT FOR MY MUM AND DAD AND MEG AND DARREN. MICHAEL TUNN, JENNY OLDERSHAW, FRANCIS LEACH, ROSIE BEATON, JASLYN HALL AND ADAM SPENCER FROM TRIPLE J. EXTRA SPECIAL THANKS TO JANE COX FOR THE CARE SHE TOOK IN PROTECTING ME. RHONDA WILLIAMS, ELAINE COOKE, DEBORAH TOBIAS AND BLAIR FOOTS FROM THE ABC. BIG THANKS TO BOB LEWIS FROM SITE SECURITY. IF YOU EVER NEED PERSONAL PROTECTION, LOOK NO FURTHER THAN BOB! MY YUM CHA PALS ELEANOR THORNTON AND NEEDEYA ISLAM. GEORGE EPAMINONDAS, LAWRIE ZION, THE BLACK FLUFFY CAT FROM NEXT DOOR WITH A PENCHANT FOR SHAVED HAM AND HELL, AND WHILE I'M AT IT, MY VERY RESOURCEFUL ACCOUNTANT BARRY FROM ENTART BUSINESS MANAGEMENT. THANK YOU TO MY SYDNEY FAMILY, TRACEY, JAMES, HENRY AND ARTHUR GALLAGHER. NICOLE, JACK, GEORGE AND IAN ROGERSON, THANK YOU FOR LETTING ME PLAY WITH YOUR BEAGLE! MY LITERARY GODMOTHER, JENNIFER DABBS, AND MISTER UNSECURED PERSONAL LOAN, ANTHONY FITZPATRICK. LYNETTE HARRISON, ANGRY YOUNG ICON SHANE PAXTON, NICHOLAS ROTHWELL, IRINA DUNN FROM THE SYDNEY WRITERS CENTRE, LYNNE HAULTAINE, MICHAEL PARISI, ANGELA BAGGIOS AND THEIR SON LUCA. GERALDINE DOOGUE, THE INIMITABLE AND GORGEOUS LISBETH GORR, INDIRA NAIDOO, SANDRA SULLY (YOUR NOTE IS PRECIOUS TO ME!) AND THE MANY MANY PEOPLE WHO WROTE OR CONTACTED ME TO OFFER SUPPORT. THANK YOU TO MY LAWYERS, BRUCE McCLINTOCK SC, PETER WERTHEIM AND MOST ESPECIALLY MICHAEL MARX OF CHALMERS MARX IN SYDNEY FOR THEIR STELLAR ASSISTANCE. ALSO, ROBBIE MACGREGOR, MATTHEW KELLY, MY SHRINK DR MICHAEL AND ANYBODY ELSE WHO WAS

NICE TO ME. OH, AND I DON'T CARE WHAT THE COOL PEOPLE SAY, ELIZABETH WURTZEL'S BOOK *PROZAC NATION* WAS LIKE AN EXOTIC, IF PROBLEMATIC, PRESENT FROM THE GODDESS! (I HOPE I LOOK THAT SEXY WHEN I'M DEPRESSED!) ENDLESS THANKS TO MY PARTNER JOHN POWELL FOR TOLERATING MY SIX MONTH LONG HISSY FIT.

TECH FOLK: MY WRITING HAS IMPROVED, I THINK, A GREAT DEAL SINCE I SHELLED OUT FOR A SEXY NEW MACINTOSH. SO I HAVE TO SAY THANKS TO PHIL KINGSMILL, ROD KIRKPATRICK AND CAMERON McDONALD STUART FROM APPLE FOR THEIR ASSISTANCE WHEN I CONTINUALLY DEMANDED 'WHAT DOES THIS BUTTON DO?' ALEX THOMAS FROM SIRIUS TECHNOLOGY PROVIDED INVALUABLE COMMUNICATIONS LITERACY. TAMSIN SMITH AND HELEN BASIC OF MICROSOFT FOR GETTING OFFICE 98 FOR MAC IN TIME FOR ME TO EDIT!

IN UNISON WITH FRACTURED AUSTRALIAN AUTHORS EVERYWHERE: THE UNUSUALLY HIP, STYLISH AND PATIENT JANE PALFREYMAN FROM RANDOM HOUSE WHO IS TIRELESS IN HER EFFORTS TO COAX DECENT PROSE. ALL THE OTHER BOFFINS FROM RANDOM TOO, ESPECIALLY THE INDUSTRIOUS BELINDA ALEXANDRA, WHO WILL ONE DAY WRITE HER NOVEL ...

CHAPTER ONE
REFUSING THE STRICTURE OF REALITY AND NURTURING THE SHIT WITHIN

Excuse me, but am I alone in assuming that history bore a MINOR progressive conceptual movement known as the Enlightenment? Admittedly, my tertiary training is as random and untamed as Pat Rafter's lavish chest rug ... but, you know, I kind of thought that we, as a complex society, had outrun the need to deposit our faith in the lap of some tarot card wielding, chakra realigning, libation pouring, Myst playing, anti-oxidant taking, relentlessly individualist imaginary wizard who reeks variously of incense, stupidity and geranium oil.

Patently, in disputing the existence of a Higher Power, I am seriously at odds with your average shiatsu masseuse. New Age Orthodoxy Be Buggered, I say as I wickedly mine the fissures in the quartz crystal of contemporary self-embrace! Not aware-ness of my rising sign nor porcelain oil burners nor intimacy with the ramblings of esteemed pamphleteer Deepak Chopra will equip me for an adequate life on this, my ailing planet. Alleged self-discovery is not the path to lasting peace. Ghan the fascinating sex dwarf will not lead you to nirvana! Spirituality is a fiction! Spurn all gurus, hirsute or no! Hey, do you really want to do anything that Demi Moore does? (Apart from snogging Bruce Willis, that is. Not that he's my type, but a bit of sweaty trade never did harm a girl. Wonder if he's seeing anyone yet?)

Have you ever considered the possibility that the multi-billion dollar self-help industry is actually a plot hatched somewhere in a dank, humourless corner of the Pentagon designed entirely to keep you dirt poor, overburdened with doubt and stupid enough to actually enjoy programs such as *Hey! Hey! It's Saturday*? Well, darn it, it's occurred to me! And that is why, in a perverse spirit of generosity, I have decided to rake the detritus from the crazy paving we recognise as human endeavour and forge a trajectory toward the One Truth: Everything's Fucked.

I cannot pinpoint the exact moment in which this simple axiom first revealed itself to me. I would like to say that my epiphany occurred on 11 November 1975 when I, as a diminutive grade scholar, learnt that the august Gough Whitlam had been relieved of his duties as Australia's Greatest Statesperson Ever by some antique constitutional glitch—with a little bit of help from some avaricious right-wing fuck-sticks, natch. Sadly, I was an underpoliticised seven year old and merely relished the opportunity to loudly chastise gaberdine-clad capitalists on the hustings without fear of parental reproach. Actually, the guiding premise for my adult intellectual life very probably found its first expression in my impressionable young colon. Each morning at assembly we queued like a calcified congregation to receive the sacrament of cow's milk, nicely warmed by the antipodean sun. As I wrestled in sick bay one sticky school day with the first of many irritable bowel incidents, I suddenly knew that there was no benign being that would holistically govern me. I recognised my citizenship in a cruel society that forced decent men out of government, mere babes to imbibe poison milk and endless repeats of *Bewitched* on weekday afternoons. (Hey, and what is it with *Bewitched* anyway? As if the systematised gynocide of millions of European alleged witches, who were, doubtless, quite useful women with fundamental obstetrics skills and handy with a placenta and the odd piece of aspirin bark, wasn't enough already! Why did Hollywood feel compelled to symbolically infibulate Samantha by making her choose formica and hetero-sexual orthodoxy over supernatural bliss? Not that I actually believe in witches, and the noisy pagans down the road with their techno and their tinkly bits really shit me. But it was a sitcom, damnit! So that's hardly the point!)

My conviction that just about all things, indeed, were resolutely fucked was nourished during the course of my adolescence. Persistent acne, the unflattering eighties advent of the tube skirt and dropped-waist frock and, significantly, the absence of premium quality cannabis in my life, all erupted as testimony to a deceptively simple realisation. Beyond my personal tawdry sphere, the wide decrepit world heaved 'neath the substantial weight of its own stinking shit. No uniform, equitable and just land rights legislation. Nuclear testing. Overt and instit-utionalised sexism. Beyond the usual catch-all leftie tote bag of complaint that I take wherever I go, *Australia's Funniest Home Video* emerged in the early nineties thereby dissolving any feeble filament of pride in nationhood or humanity I may have tenaciously clutched. Then Kurt died, Nirvana stopped making records, Courtney acquired some brand of no-carb, meek brown eyebrow pencil, tasteful lip gloss make-over borrowed straight from a hellish *New Idea* aesthete's pastel longing and I considered going into therapy for, perhaps, the fourth futile time.

As a broken, putative human who has survived a barrage

of therapeutic modalities with virtually all her neuroses intact, I am forced, I fear, to devise a new mechanism for survival. And this, comrade, is it. The compendium of hate before you is the inevitable conceptual by-product of my fruitless jousting with mystic myopic Jungian hippie dicks, colour therapists and the odd saucy palmist. I have tired of having my psyche poked, my astral envelope manipulated and my credit rating challenged. Given the energy and the dosh I have donated to the healing arts, all my supposed welts and imperfections should no longer cause me concern. The fact remains, however, that I still find the world problematic, if not unspeakably vile.

Rather obviously, I am not alone in my revulsion. One could take the view, I suppose, that individuals are basically reasonable and it is merely when they embark upon discourse and society and things that comprise the 'world' that everything's ruined. Well, frankly, I have enough solid time for postmodernity to view this foundationalist assumption as total crap. Individuals, rather than being contained, static, measurable beings are, in fact, defined entirely by their exchanges with Others. Further, they are defined in relation to what they are not. To illustrate: I am Helen Razer because I am NOT Jo-Beth Taylor, Burt Reynolds or a bunch of freshly picked English mint. Or something. Where was I? (Damn that Jacques Derrida and his ideas of eternally reson-ating difference. I haven't got the time to not coincide with my imagined immediate presence, or whatever. I think I'll just get back to roundly despising everybody. To address the question of whether we are absent, unravelled, complex selves or just cheeky knowable monkeys is not here our concern. I just want to get through life with dignity, pride and the simple knowledge that I have never constructed a sentence employing the prefix 'My clairvoyant says'.)

The more popular view (Hey! what could be more popular than drowning in the postmodern impasse?) of course is that the world is absolute HEAVEN and it's just our fault that we don't coincide with all the dippy fun that's out there to be had. Deepak, Louise Hay and all their turdy mates want us to believe that their stinky, dumb books and CD-ROMs and what not can effect some kind of literary lobotomy. Well, sure, if you want to be a hard-body dotard with no sense of civic responsibility, that's just grand. We who intone the single, fractious, liberating mantra, Everything's Fucked, know better!

It is vital to acquire and acknowledge evidence that just about all things are shithouse regularly. We will deal with the specifics of this daily antinihilistic ritual in coming chapters. Some people have a very lean database of stuff to hate, so I will also provide you, the petulant patient, with a starter kit of fucked things to think about and a general Crankiness Template. It is essential to remember, as long as you retain decent manners and never vote for the Coalition or the One Nation party, that you are not entirely to blame.

Beyond my patented Anatomy of Healthy Hating, I will also attempt to assist you in fixating obsessively on a variety of decent things in the case of you undergoing a postfoundationalist identity emergency. These will include, naturally, the *Two Fat Ladies*, the early selected writings of Julie Burchill, Rock, Noodles and Residents for Reconciliation.

Importantly, I wish also to offer the studious malcontent a series of watertight excuses for his/her misanthropy. We shall examine phenomena such as immaturity, indolence and rage in their broader social contexts. It's *okay* to act like a complete dick in specific cases. On occasion, as you shall see, overt dickiness is both your responsibility and right as a besieged, intelligent citizen.

In this, your passage to authentic and embittered recovery, we'll meet a host of despicable infidels and together, perhaps, we'll devise ways to embarrass the bejesus out of them. On that note, I will also offer my Treatise On The Origin Of Human Smugness and chronicle ways in which you can use both cynicism and stylish lethargy to your best advantage. We will learn to love our sarcasm, my scepticism and desire *not* to be bothered by breezy social gatherings on a Sunday afternoon.

As indicated previously, this work derives its motivation from the scores of plain evil, stump-dumb and dull charlatan healers out there in dystopia that would have you blaming, damning and rebuilding your lovely selves entirely. We shall learn to recognise our enemies and to seek and destroy their unctuous influence. We shall begin to act as unswervingly ethical guardians when our fraught and misguided friends would rather consult a bag of frigging rocks with pictures on them than *you* to aid them in watershed decision making. *Oh, will I continue my mutually destructive relationship, will I reconcile with my mother despite our fraught history, will I transform my career path? I don't know.* LET ME CHECK MY LITTLE RUNES!! AAARGH. We will picket against rebirthers, we will drain flotillas of float tanks and we will NOT anthropomorphise dolphins! We will hit this fundamentally flawed ill with unrepentant, full-core systemic fungicide! Did somebody say crystal healing? Or did somebody say fuck off, thanks, I think I'll actually activate my hitherto sluggish synapses instead? We will not sit idly by as colleagues fall vulnerable victim to the barely articulate admonitions of soothsaying sibyls with a couple of shitty old coins and a few words of imitation Mandarin that wouldn't buy you a steamer of gow gee at yum cha! We will not tolerate the selective, insensitive acculturation of south-east Asian societies by well-fed middlebrow middleclass Caucasians who are too bloody lazy to take their hands off of their well-affricated genital mound for five minutes so as they could enrol in a course for java-script web design or something actually fucking useful.

If it's fine with you, and you wouldn't rather spend your time trying out Quake II cheats, taking risks with dangerous pizza or amending your totally fictitious CV, we'll get things started. I'd like to dismantle the garish vehicles driven by New Age Travellers in my first rumination. (I haven't quite exorcised my anger yet.)

And remember, you are entirely not to blame! Oh, if you hate people or things simply because of their race, creed, dress sense, physical ability, difference or general social coordinates, then you are entirely to blame and should never have bought this text in the first instance. I recommend that anyone who has ever said, 'You know, people criticise her; but Pauline Hanson makes a lot of sense!' should spend all their money AT ONCE on a comprehensive New Age so-called humanist library and then choke on their own noisome self-indulgent ideological waste product. I guess I should say I recommend hating untenable belief systems and *not* actual people! All clear? Friends again? You are not entirely to blame!

CHAPTER TWO
NEW AGEISM
FOR FUN
& PROFIT

The first glaring thing that strikes me about these people is that they're really dumb. I know, I know. However, some simple truths bear constant restatement. If I may return, shakily, to the history of western thought, with adamant apologies to my first year philosophy tutors. There was, as mentioned previously, if cautiously, the Enlightenment. Bang! (Sort of.) A widespread realisation, starting, I think, with that francophone fruit-bat Descartes that all men (*sic*) are capable of 'rational' thought and are indeed, require to postulate energetically about their reason for existing. As many have ventured this century, if you don't count the syphilitic and obtuse Friedrich Nietzsche (he was way too clever far before his time), there are a lot of big delectable holes to be poked in concepts such as rationalism and logic and first principles and shit like that. Incidentally, Fred was the person who recognised, named and deconstructed the concept of Primary Nihilism. The belief lazy people have in God, or whatever. Look it up if you have the time! (It's nasty and fun!) However, may I be amongst those who intone Don't Walk Away Renee. (I apologise! I've been waiting to use that gag for quite some time now.) In any case, zip mode forward some three centuries or such and, from what I understand, those amazing French people are *still* arguing about the shape and/or construction of reality! Seemingly, clever men and women at the Sorbonne remain entangled in a fabulous dispute about the stuff of self, knowledge, text, Jo-Beth Taylor, Burt Reynolds and mint leaves. Frankly, Michel Foucault's *The Order Of Thing*s gave me nightmares; *Disseminations* made me fractured and incomprehensible for weeks, and Julia Kristeva just brings me out in hives. However, there's always Cliff's cheat notes. And the fact remains, although these New Age Prognosticians claim to be genuinely interested in the order or 'nature' of things, there's a fuck-load of books that they haven't even bothered to read yet. These pagan wannabes don't even begin to problematise their own existence, much less take a good hard look at their ridiculous manner of dressing! So, hippie, read some Deleuze and then tell me whether you're Being, Becoming or just Being A Dick.

One of the first problems with these reincarnated wildebeests in caftans is that they seem to uniformly believe that You Are Responsible For Your Own Destiny. Therefore, according to their own silky parameters, women don't have many jobs in middle management simply because they don't feel like it, folk of the Islamic faith in the former Yugoslav Republic are knocked off because that's what they like to do on their days off; and indigenous Australians don't have shit because, HEY! that's what they deserve. Well, bollocks, actually. Can I just impart patriarchy, latter-day crusades and radical racism here? Well, I could say that, but that would a typical karmically imbalanced response from a poorly reincarnated centaur who is still pissed off that she had to endure a lifetime with the gonads of a horse. (Oh, the things the wood nymphs said to me on the way home from pony club!)

Obviously, hungry kiddies in Somalia aren't just reanimated anorexic princesses from South Yarra and obviously my rubber parts are of quite a modest size, thank you. A thornier problem, however, is encountered when we attempt to deconstruct the foundationalism so essential to a New Age 'philosophy'. As with many Christians, logicians and seventies-style 'swingers', these hippie shits cling rather desperately to a certain presupposition upon which all further crackpottery is heaped. (Swingers allow The Climax to function as God, if you're wondering. They're a singularly plain bunch of people ... people, have you noticed that too?) To be honest, I don't know if I'm capable of defining their flimsy New Age premise. It seems to vary from nut to nut. Whether it is something along the lines of 'all human beings are plugged into the cosmic grid, baby, and spiritually attached to Mother Earth' or some more prosaic pre-Socratic notion like 'we are all made out of stuff' I'm not really sure. Maybe they think that we'll all die if we don't eat textured vegetable protein. Whatever. I'm just saying that I think it's simultaneously possible to believe firmly in no Final Authority or Founding Principle and to be a decent human. I reckon it might even be desirable to relinquish one's faith in certain 'natural' essentialist 'facts'. But that's just me. Next!

Another thing that is resoundingly shitty about these people with their Aleister Crawley diagrams is that they don't seem to give a toss about who they pinch stuff from. You know, I'm A Little Bit Tantric, I'm A Little Bit Rock And Roll. Well, admittedly I'm capable of enjoying the music of Skinny Puppy as well as Led Zeppelin. It's good to be diverse. However, I did pay the recommended retail of $29.95 for each of my CDs. So, I ask, when was the last time Io The Feckless Psychic sent the Grand Chant Master money for a new saffron robe? Or, more to the point, actively censured the Chinese government for its continued unwelcome presence in Tibet? At the very least, many Australian God-bots actually feed people, even if they do make them listen to that awful Jesus music on nylon string guitars. And where was the Australian Psychics Association when rural churches bravely challenged John Howard's Wik Bill? They were off getting an aromatherapy treatment, I'd wager. And then they'd probably return to herbal infusions served in clay pinch-pots with diagrams nicked from a Balinese spiritual lexicon which they bought while eco-touristing in fucking Indonesia, never giving a thought to the East Timorese, and then, post citronella tea, began to engage in some insipid whitey crypto-imperialist conversation about how they were going to combine their Siberian-inspired Shamanic Voyaging (what Gulag?) Service with Australian indigenous dreamtime mythology while SOME LITTLE BALDING PRICK WAS TRYING TO EXTINGUISH NATIVE TITLE! And what were they doing about it? Apart from exercising cynical, condescending, true colonial exploitation, dick all. It's just not cool to nick stuff from cultures other than your own without paying for it properly. Sometimes a libation just isn't enough, hippies.

Quite apart from violating five third-world cultures in a single afternoon, these people are responsible for creating a niche market for New Age music. Now, there is a place for a stitch of the Orb, Tricky or even The Aphex Twin in my own time. But, you know, enough is enough and sometimes you just really NEED to play *Back in Black*. I used to really enjoy getting facials until every beauty salon became an 'aesthetic therapist', replaced my favourite chemical peel with essential oils that give me a rash and started piping dinky Orca The Stupid Fat Whale Seaside Music through w-bins next to my ears. This diffident ooze attacks me at every turn and succeeds in only making me want to piss. And who is this ditzy Rapunzel shit called Enya? When is she going to choke on a poison apple? Why does some slappable skinny brunette slag who managed to stop sticking her fingers down her throat just long enough to learn how to use some substandard sequencing software have to whine about cock-sucking green fields and clouds and the western European goddess tradition every time I go and eat in a restaurant. There's a burial mound, baby, in County Meath and it's got your stupid name on it. Enya! I'd rather listen to Bill Wyman's solo album. I'd rather eat mystic dolphin poos. Nothing, not even Italian house remixes of Celine Dion dueting with Michael Bolton with solos by Kenny G, John Tesh and Yianni with lyrics by Alanis 'Isn't It Ironic Not!' Morisette, makes me so livid and full of acrid tension.

New Age books are crap and insubstantial and no fun. Ditto for their food. And as if it wasn't enough that a legion of spectacularly unsuccessful baby boomers taint the suburbs with screeds of shit prose in dream diaries, incense boats, rose crystal birdie mobiles and lurid pictures of the Hindu Goddess Kali tacked onto their fleshless refrigerators with iridescent Magic Happens magnets, the youngsters are at it also! In my inner-city suburb, a formerly pleasant locale where chirpy lads once treated their good ladies to beer bongs before exiting on skateboards to the nearest fashionably feculent fleshpot for a robust dose of alterna-noise, there are presently no less than twenty naturopathy practices! (Now, don't misread me. Western medical orthodoxy needs to be challenged, having accrued over some thirty years a litany of complaints able to rival in length Bill Gates' fiscal acquisitions for last week. I'm just painting a picture!) Where once were dank little head shops purveying honest hash pipes and

Bob Marley T-shirts, there is now only the derisive glow of New Age boutiques boasting books with names like *Hug The Monster*, pop-up versions of the Kama Sutra, garrulous crap artists talking on vile C90 cassettes about how I can meditate my excess weight off, plastic I-Ching coins and more bloody crystals. Exotic tanneries and delightful gaming parlours have given way to purveyors of irksome, fundamentally evil New Age pap. How groovy, I ask you, does any inner suburb remain when a girl can't buy a simple monogrammed studded leather cock ring for her intended or beloved?? My suburb was once salty and hard and full of the kicking promise of angry youth. It is now diluted and flaccid and full of complacent little shits who knock on my door if I choose to pump *Death In Vegas* up to an audible level. And here again, the New Age boomer-nots have supplanted civic integrity for extreme self-regard. Not one self-professed 'urban tribe' denizen attended our residents' action group emergency strategy meeting. It was only nice, sensible single mothers with decent, wholesome Marxian proclivities who gave a shit about our zoning code being violated by a topless bar AND an unlicensed textile sweatshop! Well, as long as the proposed establishments did not impede the progress of our friendly neighbourhood ley lines, I guess they didn't mind. The thing that marks them as particularly horrid is that they appear to drop acid religiously. It is my opinion that psychedelics constitute some pretty serious neuron-devouring shit. However, if you wish to rebelliously impede your intelligence, your vocabulary and your chances of ever engaging in any meaningful discourse at all, go ahead! Take a whole foolscap folder! You're only frying your own logic board and providing amusement for me at the supermarket while you giggle at the eggs. Outlandishly enough, however, the New Age toddlers seem to disregard the hard lessons learnt in the sixties and, quite openly, enjoy religious experiences at turnstiles, pedestrian crossings and median strips. I do not want my suburb littered by you acid munching, higher power seeking human blotting paper! Go out and get *HardWare* on video like a normal drug-pig and be circumspect and don't go outside!

The other of my favourite places that has been systematically populated by these little shits is the binary realm. We had to listen to them bang on about virtual reality! We had to be embarrassed to enjoy unravelling Riven in case the shop attendant mistook us for a plainclothes ditz! And now the little fuckers are all over the Net! In my favourite chat rooms! Colonising the Philosophy & Culture boards with their needless prattle! My passion for my PowerMac 9600 is tarnished by the exchanges I am forced to endure. *Wow, technology is how we're going to return to Mother Earth. Computers will help us reunite with our alienated tree frog spirit.* No! Computers are where I will learn HTML, gain fruitful employment and regularly reassess my frequent flyer points. And while I'm at it, techno does not resonate with the ancient heartbeat of a beautiful planet in need of our healing love. It's something that makes sense to people in spangly hotpants that are absolutely fucked up on tatty year eight science project amphetamines that I wouldn't have the heart to kill vermin with. ARE WE CLEAR ON THIS? Computers are fabulous toys and CJ Bolland is merely a Belgian who makes music for people who take way too much Sudafed.

The worst thing about all of them: they take your money! They're only marginally cheaper than an accredited psychotherapist and, generally speaking, much easier to get an appointment with at short, needy notice. Further, despite the avowed New Age belief in the individual wresting absolute competent control of his or her destiny, a saccharine simpering clairvoyant is much less likely than, say, your average Lacanian-Freudian analyst to angrily (and, doubtless, in a Viennese accent) accuse you of wet pre-Oedipal indolence, prescription drug dependence and a general disinterest in your eventual talking cure. I concede, in my gormless, vulnerable past, I did consult a psychic! When all I really needed was a good root and a new frock, I took my sad, shameful self to a den of New Age chicanery and allowed myself to be immersed in the gentleman's 'revelations'. These Amazing Insights included 'You're very passionate about politics and have left-wing tendencies.' He just may have been tipped off by my Subvert The Dominant Paradigm T-shirt, the copy of *Das Kapital* on my lap or the essential Bolshy leisuretime projectile which I eventually decided to hurl in his impassive direction ... a smoking Molotov cocktail! (It's a rich fantasy life.) But who am I to judge?

I'll tell you who I am to judge, hippie! I'm a decent citizen with occasional weaknesses that have been mined and exploited by you and your irksome coconspirators! I'm a resident of a formerly quaint locale that has been rapaciously colonised, ravaged and scarred by you and now looks like a porpoise-scudded post New Age apocalyptic Kuwait! I'm an active constituent with a well-developed sense of circumspect civic pride who despairs for the public intellectual life of her country! In the conceptual spaces where once we argued the viability of applied poststructuralism over beer, we now bear the torment of your treatise on the relational structure of the Ascendant Sign with a Sixth Node between your swinish gulps of gluten-reduced soy smoothies. You are corrupting our youth, imbuing even their simple weekend pleasure of progressive, syncopated techno with the threat of your vile spirituality. You are infiltrating our beauty salons! I can't even have a simple pedicure without the word 'reflexology' being wielded like a rusty harbinger of the New Age gloom that will surely envelop the world if you are not thwarted in your covetous quest to ruin everything. Valuable shelf space in public libraries is wolfishly devoured by your lean, mangy instructional manifestos. Gorgeous black dresses with astrakhan trim are no longer available at my favourite shops. No! Amorphous sacks of indeterminate colour that rob the impoverished modern Spiritually Enlightened bosom of attention are all that I can buy. Formerly raffish waiters who once sweet-talked me into ordering way too much vodka and saturated fat now remonstrate when I plead for nonorganic fettucine carbonara and then administer their advice on liver cleansing, the marvel that is Spirulina and how, if I just loved myself a little bit more, I could slim down to a karmically cautious size eight.

Frankly, my patience is at its logical end. I've had my fill of the New Age's brittle Lenten onanism. I don't even find the hippies funny any more. Further, carob-coated rice cakes never tasted good in the first place. What is to be done? An alleged therapeutic community has done us authentic neurotics naught but harm. Perhaps the counterculture of the sixties was thoroughly altruistic. Perhaps, in the beginning, they actually meant well! In the contemporary climate, however, the rasion d'etre of the New Age seems to be to take my money and piss me off!

Well, I rather think we've expended sufficient energetic attention on the tie-dyed foibles of the demi-druids, don't you? We'll leave them for the moment to their pitiful white robery, stationary sex and humming workshops. Off they pop with their rattan shopping baskets groaning to contain a booty of misappropriated trinkets from oppressed ethnic groups! Up they go with their supposedly hygienic vital organs, their cypress oil and their angel therapists! Away they amble to their prefab yurts, their detestable 'music' and, to paraphrase the expression of a valiant anti-New-Age poet activist, to holiday in someone else's misery. Salute them with your middle finger as they toddle toward a steaming tepee in which they will place their toothless faith. They will dream of feeling up Enya. They will decant their faith and hope into a bottle of lavender essence, rather than trying to participate in affairs of state or democracy. They can have their stinking bourgeois revolution and their brown rice sushi! And we can outrun their noxious influence! Let us begin to compile our more autonomous, robust and sexy charter for exceeding despair! READY?

CHAPTER THREE
AN ANATOMY OF HEALTHY
HATING

My grandfather has been apoplectic with rage for, I venture, seventy hard years. As a consequence, he has turned what I believe to be a permanent and unflattering shade of pinkish violet. Petrifying high-octane anger has consumed him whole. He has arrived at a passage in this fractured narrative of a life where he is only capable of conversing with early evening television news broadcasts, specific AM talk radio stations and a disinterested and effete family cat. His most frequently offered critique would seem to be 'Oowargh, whadya mean?' His only form of discourse is the monologue. The point, dear reader, is that I have no wish for you to grow up embittered, purple and friendless like Grumpy Pop. However, a cautious and clever Hate Management System may reward you with untold success!

Most citizens, as my mother would gratefully acknowledge, are not like my grandfather at all. Rather, they appear to endure life with a steadfastly cloying, Pollyannaesque demeanour that is only marginally less nasty and just as carcinogenic as my forebear's. Animosity, when it is tentatively expressed from the covert steaming internal urn of an average human's baleful anxiety, is usually sugar-coated and reserved, somewhat oddly, for their 'inferiors'. This unctuous habit is observed easily in the manner of a gaudy female frock-shop attendant. Eager to assert her meretricious authority she will gush gush with utterances such as, 'I don't think we have that in your size', and further enacting her rotten, clumsy style of subterfuge she suggests, 'Why don't you wear a brightly coloured scarf or a chunky bracelet to draw attention away from your PARCHMENT THIGHS, GARGANTUAN HIPS AND YOUR REPUGNANT SPOTTY VISAGE.' The hair architect or, as murmured previously, the modern salon de beaute can prove a demoralising journey. On a recent deep-suburban sojourn, I was in need of a manicure. When I asked, prettily and coyly, to have my nails augmented with the undoubtedly standard and lovely enamel Rouge-Noir, I was eyed and roundly despised with beauty scholar pertness. The hermetically-sealed taupe empress snarled at me and virtually called me a cheap slut. 'Why don't you take a French polish' came one inane solution. Urgh! Bookshop attendants are also notoriously snobbish and waiters are always eager to correct your, quite acceptable, methods of pronunciation. Frankly, I think if I am prepared to shell out anything over fifteen bucks for a bottle of wine, I can perform whatever elaborate tongue gymnastics I choose. All visitors to any digital emporium will surely identify a crypto-fascist of a similar order. 'Well, yesss,' begins the soggy Bill Gates wannabe, his acrid perspiration stains encroaching from under his pallid arms and threatening to conquer every micro-fibrous stitch of his promotional Windows '95 T-shirt. 'Flash ROM is a difficult mechanism to understand, I suppose. But I guess I couldn't expect anyone who doesn't know any DOS commands to really have total certainty about their modem choice.' Well, take your ISP, shove it where even Microsoft employees don't wash and just sell me a fucking computer so I can go home and download some porn.

In any case, most folk amble through life with almost belligerent glee. They choose to hurt only the resolutely vulnerable, timid and chubby and then rarely summon their itinerant anger when it would prove most useful. The healthy, ruddy, classical Hate evinced by such folks as the ribald, wretchedly rude and piss funny Roman satirist Juvenal remains antique and submerged in the manufactured silt of our needlessly euphemistic age. Restore the marble ruins, I say, and begin to employ your circumspect hatred tactically and competently, rather than simply as a means to shit people who really don't deserve it.

The taut and perky couturier, the aggressive Nazi computer store binary geek and the fat tongued tri-headed Cerebrean lunk who just can't perceive the logic in allowing your unimpeded entry into his apocryphal 'ladies drink free until ten' nightclub. These people demonstrate the very antithesis of the behaviour we strive here to responsibly enact! I seek to provide aid in your commendable quest to act as a thorough psycho hose-beast when necessary. It is probable that, at this juncture in your fraught personal history, your innate talent for admonishing the guilty is occluded by a misguided sense of propriety. You must eclipse your desire to remain cosily taciturn or to be unproductively snippy. You will learn to preserve your most outlandish tirades, schemes and conceptual browneyes for the insufferable humans that so richly need your unapologetic badness! The unchecked derision of the downtrodden merely assists in bolstering an ugly, increasingly untenable situation of class warfare. Frankly, I'm amazed that this didn't occur to Karl Marx and Friedrich Engels. Perhaps if it had, Uncle Joe Stalin wouldn't have had such impudence, scorn and bad manners! Scores of Siberians would have been saved. Lenin would have been an infinitely chiller guy and Leon Trotsky wouldn't have ended up with a rather uncalled for icepick in his back. (I always wondered if there was a Menshevik subtext in *Basic Instinct*.) In any case, perhaps they should have spent a little less time worrying about revolution, alienation from one's labour and the feminisation of poverty, and included a short treatise on Just Being Nice Versus Synthesised Free Market Nastiness in the *Communist Manifesto*. They could have called it Petulance Fetishism. But, you know, I heard that Karl Marx was a rarely bathing grump who liked to commodify his pleasure in the form of cut-rate London prostitutes. Possibly too much to ask of our socialist progenitors. Whatever.

At present in this, our contemporary economy of extreme and unnecessary bitchiness, efficient hate functions like power. If we can invert the current relation of haughty despiser to marginalised despised, I'm reasonably certain that a medium sized and relatively joyous revolution would be born. Or, at the very least, we might be able to buy size twelve dresses, redistribute the wealth and topple the evil, fatuous and glistening multimedia feudal province of Nasty Baron Rupert Murdoch. Ooh, what a scrummy dream.

Needless to impart, sterling reader, hate is an awesomely complex concept. It is employed and usurped by manifold means. There is, first, a fearful, awesome, reluctantly respectful and institutionalised hate. This mode of hate is transferred, without success, upwards and tends to give its hate-smith ulcers, eczema and angst. This is the kind of hate that I, at one artless point in my life, used to have for lawyers, journalists and doctors. Until I grew up and realised that the vast majority of these alleged professional custodians of truth came from rich inbred families and talked, for the most part, through their retentive high-income-earning rectums. Before the happy industrial-era advent of trade unionism, many workers had this kind of confused, stultifying contempt for their bosses. Many, I suspect, still do. This kind of hate is not, by any means, unjustified. It's just a massive waste of time. The hate dissolves in the thin upper atmosphere before it reaches its goal. (Ooh, very Bolshy socialist realistic poetic of me, I'm impressed! I'm buggering off to write a sonnet about my scythe and the blood of workers now.)

There is, then, the less substantial, more obtuse and difficult to define free-form exchange of hate. This is the kind of honeyed hate purveyed by strumpet bulimic shop assistants and what not as documented previously. In one reading, this unruly mode of hate is promulgated to make the bearer feel better about his or her shitty life. It is a less toxic duplicate of the ubiquitous hate that emanates down from above, to be examined shortly.

Frankly, kids, both of these initial forms tend to render the hater inarticulate, unbecomingly puce with rage and ultimately impotent. Tsk tsk.

Finally there is the hate that residents of Toorak and Vaucluse bear for the rest of the crumbling, addled world. This, without doubt, takes a cooler, more condensed, elite and contained shape. It is almost as if the nation's prosperous and well-fed folk were whisked off to Switzerland at birth to have their capacity for hate cryogenically frozen. (Cryogenic freezing, as I learnt recently on the Discovery Channel, is a process which enables a more even, durable and stress-free molecular structure. Apparently it even works on disposable razors, panty-hose and trombones!) These people preserve a code of hate that is at once disdainful, detached and condescending. Hate to the privileged is golden, apotheosised and very comfy indeed upon its Mercy Seat. It's their secret! If we, the lumpen mass, can borrow from their steady born-to-fucking-rule example and combine this wintry nastiness with a couple of really cool insults, then I'm sure we'll all be well set on the rails of diesel-powered recovery.

Exceeding pedestrian animus and appropriating the icy spite of the rich is all very well and good. How does one go about utilising it? Hmmm. Well, I have a motley theory: reality is little more than an accidental waste product excreted by the omniscient, crushing mill of language. 'Expression' and 'representation' cannot genuinely refer to humanity or reality, as language itself has forged these objects. As Roland Barthes said (or was it someone else?), before he was unconditionally squashed by a Parisian laundry truck in an instant of pure existential cruelty: there ain't no such beast as a Thing In Itself. All 'things' are codified. Gender, power and couscous (which I'm sure Albert Camus ate a lot of before he was unconditionally squashed by an Algerian oncoming vehicle in an instant of pure existential cruelty) are all 'side effects' of language. (Maybe it wasn't a laundry truck. Have you ever noticed how French philosophers unwittingly choose spectacular modes of death?) Look, I didn't pay much attention when I was reading this stuff, but I do understand that language is key. (Yep, that's the kind of blunted knowledge I'm paying my HECS debt for. Sad, isn't it?)

Having established that we have merely talked our way into existence, we'll stop with the embarrassing epistemology and agree, at least, that we need to bullishly wield the eternally incisive weaponry of words in order to retain relatively good control of our mental health. If we wish to alter the architecture of our clumsy hatred, books are a fabulous place to start. I recommend the immediate purchase of a decent thesaurus and a thuddingly thick etymological dictionary. By these means you can mine concepts that have a look, resonance and history that is pleasing to your individual needs. You can begin to transform the inadequate technology of your hate rather quickly when you surmise words and concepts like chagrin, enmity and displeasure. Rancour, malevolence and asperity are also lexical fun just waiting to be had! Beyond establishing your finely attenuated palette of disease, a hard-core vocab is useful not only in helping you mentally articulate the calibre of your hate. It can really piss off horrible people! As a child who shunned sports and glitzy playground society, I found that words of any complexity more profound than 'delicatessen' really confused my classmates and provided adequate pest control. I find the same thing occurs textually when I'm partaking in a spot of IRC online drivel. Folk become frightened at your ability to revel in the endless play of language. And they tend not to give you too much shit!

Once you have grappled with the basics of Language and Knowledge and Power and all that clever clogs French concomitant garbage, you can begin to effectively combine your consummately dilly new toys. Anybody can become a garrulous, disingenuous windbag. Anybody can learn sexy new words. The trick lies in their confluence. One has to learn how to creatively lubricate the machinery of language for best effect. One must jam judiciously. It's not enough to merely improve your vocabulary in the fashion of the *Reader's Digest*. (Am I alone in suspecting this publication of conspiratorial ultraright ubermensch leanings?) A boy or girl must speak with texture, conviction and playful prudence or they'll sound like somebody's inane uncle. Marshalling technique is only temporarily sexy. Speaking in the manner of an Irrational Artiste will win you untold presence. To illustrate: daggy session musician Joe Satriani is a well-respected guitarist. Boy, can that chappie play! He's been on tour with Mick Jagger, solos like he's been genetically enhanced with three extra fingers and he knows his pentatonic scale as intimately as I am able to trace the topography of my arse cellulite. Keith Richard, by contrast, is possibly a bit of a lethargic player. But, really, who wrote 'Sympathy For The Devil'? Hmmm? My favourite Glimmer Twin can do in four notes what his ephemeral replacement will never achieve. He is tasteful, junkyard dog dirty and, above all, one of rock's most eloquent players. Joe Satriani, on the other hand, recorded *Surfing With The Fucking Alien* which, frankly, I wouldn't use as a beer coaster. Joe Satriani can be seen represented in two dimensional cardboard cutout mode in silly music shops. While the venerable Doctor Hunter S Thomson writes paeans to Keith's greatness. One player jabbers on endlessly and is remarkable only for his mathematical ingenuity. Keith's simple blues riffing on 'Monkey Man' makes me heave with emotion, SOB, and says more to me than most any man ever has! Economy and style are as important in speech as they are in rock or a Honda hatchback.

So, you have marshalled the intricacies of language! Practise your new certitude on a house pet. Write officious missives to your local federal representative. Or, if you do not feel ready to challenge an impaired democracy, experiment with imperious notes to the suburban newspaper or angry demands to inadequate manufacturers of confectionery. Remain steadfast in your quest to distil your anger and loathing into a tolerable, readable form. It helps to cry out sensibly! (It also helps to eat cookie-dough ice-cream, to enjoy indulgent foot baths and to dexterously masturbate in a pure soothing envelope of premium quality, clean and fluffy flannelette sheets.)

With this armoury of new outrageous hope, you are now able to systematise your hate. As stated in this monograph's introductory passages, I recommend the ritual realisation of one's grievances through text (which begins to explain why I occasionally write books, I suppose). Begin by making a list. I am thinking of calling the people at Filemaker Pro so that they can include a Hate Template in their newest relationship database version, possibly with active links to good cranky websites. For the moment, however, a pen and paper will suffice. In the approximate order of the degree to which they really get on your wick, inscribe a list of irksome things. Now, mentally cross-reference this list with your ability to access and confront the people, corporations or things that really shit you. If, for example, you are pissed off with the Time Warner corporation for their questionable decision to excise many Gangsta Rap artists from their catalogue, then maybe you can cross that off. Unless you have Ted Turner's private email address, or you're a really together astroturf lobbyist, you might not actually be able to do anything. In any case, with a clear practical head, revise your list. Plan opportunities in which you might confront your oppressors. Always examine the origin of your discontent intimately! For example, if native fauna really rubs you up wrong simply because you have a negative 'thing' about marsupials, you may want to rethink your proclivities. Oh, and revise the list at least once a week. If you cannot devise at least three new demons, then large parts of your brain are temporarily malfunctioning. If this is the case, I recommend a high protein meal followed by an hour or two of goddamn Riven topped off by an assiduous wrangle with a quality broadsheet. This usually wakes me up. The next chapter will also provide the promised Hate Starter Kit. Further, always compile your list at work, if you are actually still employed and have not become one of the Coalition government's disenfranchised youngsters. This will make you feel all covert and naughty. When you have successfully and rationally confronted your oppressors, if funds permit, buy yourself a new pair of PVC boots, a nice seed bell for the local rosellas or a dirty book. Reward yourself: You have done very well.

In this chapter, I wish to fiendishly misappropriate the quick-fix style of self-help 'literature' and provide you with a list.

HELEN'S NEVER FAIL FIVE POINT PLAN FOR THWARTING SHIT-HEADS

1

Hate. Know your enemy. Using, when required, tools such as macro-economic theory, the anatomy of desire or the history of colonisation in Australia (for example), calmly work out who you really hate. It is pivotal to remember that you are not entitled to hate people merely because they (a) possess something that you want, (b) have a social history, inherited creed or genealogy of which you illogically disapprove, or (c) are vegetarians. The latter preclusion can, admittedly, prove a challenge. In any case, hard as it is, try not to be a total sententious prick.

2

Read. Absorb some Roland Barthes, and many other books without pictures or big writing. (If you do find out how Roland really did die, feel at liberty to email me: helenrazer@triplej.abc. net.au.) Even the barest working knowledge of some solid contemporary hypotheses can significantly embellish both your confidence and ability to efficiently deal with crap. I, for example, know virtually nothing. The minute understanding I can boast, however, has turned me into the supremely egoistic and comfortably opinionated revolutionary behemoth I am today. Seriously, though, the odd joust with Jacques can provide invaluable exercise. In being able to competently pinpoint the theoretical origins of others' dangerous stupidity, it is easier to navigate your way back to a sheltered place by means of philosophical triangulation.

3

Flounce. Be clever, regal and a little bit impassive when confronting idiots. Embrace the Princess or Princey within. Glamour can be calming. Think about what colour to paint your toenails. Rehearse saying 'Fourteen tiger chips on red, Harry, and make it snappy!' You may also wish to attempt some prudent swooning. (The purchase and strategic placement of a Louis XIV reproduction chair is recommended to augment and soften this act.) Summon the images of Sean Connery's Bond, Grace Kelly's every delectable portrayal or the unshakable poise of crusty Harvey Keitel, who even survived *Sister Act* with his integrity intact. Waft about randomly, own something diaphanous (even if you're a bloke) and practise a controlled and aesthetically cautious form of melancholy. Include the terms 'creature', 'casino' and 'chemise' in everyday conversation. Read some more books.

4

Recount. Make the list! As often as possible, recount your recent wrangles with obtuse people and systems. Again, use this opportunity to revise the legitimacy of your complaint.

5

Never Trust A Hippie. Some truths bear restating …

Hate. Read. Flounce. Recount. And smash the New Age. We are now ready to move on to the next phase in embroidering our fabulous discontent.

CHAPTER FOUR

CIRCUMSPECT LOATHING FOR THE TIMID

The pitiful truth about some diffident citizens is that they just seem to want to hug the world. Or, if they do not adore absolutely everything, they devote their fervid, misguided energy to finding the wrong things abhorrent. In no other person is this latter transgression more acutely exemplified than Pauline Hanson. Her peculiar mind macarenas feverishly with cause and effect. Some profound neural dysfunction enables her to hold indigenous Australians, multiculturalism, ABC journalists and hard words that she, poor possum, just doesn't understand, entirely account-able for her frustrations. Of course, if she were to simply and miraculously stop being Stupid Duplicitous Spice for just a millisecond, she just might be able to locate the real origin of her elephantine unhappiness. Pauline has problematised the world all wrong! She needs to address questions such as: why didn't I receive a comprehensive education? How can I, as a moderately successful businesswoman, acquire the diligent work ethic and the sense of community personified by my south-east Asian comrades? Or, significantly, why has the Revlon consortium stopped producing fuchsia glitter cream eye-colour?

The Oxley Moron myopically blaming Aboriginal activists for the nation's woes makes about as much lucid sense as American parents blaming silverchair for their progeny's bad behaviour. First, indigenous Australians have been way too occupied since 1788 getting killed, marginalised and systematically abused to cause any significant 'trouble'. Second, silverchair are a nice group of lads from Newcastle. I have had the enviable fortune of meeting them and their parents. They are about as capable of inspiring Teen Unrest as I would be of emulating Kate Fischer's adipose charms on the *Bugs Bunny Show*.

An intimate knowledge of your personal discontent is desirable. However, as we have discussed, you must acquire the instruments that will allow you to accurately define it. A prehensile mind and an aerobicised tongue are essential lifestyle accessories. You don't want to be like Pauline, do you?

So, you've done the Never Fail Five Point Plan, imbibed your sluggish Soy Health Tiger Shake and marshalled the mystery of the coloured stones puzzle on the top of the Golden Dome. (Please! If you have any Riven cheats for me—I'm going gradually insane!) All these steps toward Patented Razer Health have been dutifully completed and you still don't know what to dislike! Naturally, one has to organically drift toward one's own antipathies. Aversion is just as important and unswervingly personal as love. I do not profess expertise in determining the natural course of another citizen's displeasure! However, perhaps you may like to first try emulating some of my suggestions. Once you have a feel for recognising dissonance, vacuity and scum, you can begin to devise your own Litany Of Loathing. Please apply the following Crankiness Template liberally.

1. Demi Moore. Although I have avowed my scorn for

GI Jane repeatedly and in various media, she just won't go away. Whether it's the result of intensive reconstructive surgery or wheat-grass colonic irrigation, she continually returns to full feminine elasticity after the birth of each of her fourteen children. In the unlikely case that I should ever choose to procreate, I am certain that I would become stupendously large, indolent and disdainful of society. Demi, however, runs with coltish alacrity to the next multimillion dollar flick that requires her full or partial nudity. Is this correct post-partum decorum? I think not. Even if she is one of those rare antibody-enhanced creatures who is never burdened with physical ill, flab or inadequacy, she should, for the sake of the sisterhood, at least pretend to have a weight problem. There is also the matter of Planet Hollywood. Why does anyone who can green-light an odious piece of shit like *Striptease* and demand a reported twelve million bucks for her trouble need any more money? Can't she quietly invest in a software company if she's that fucking greedy? Why do we non-Americans have to wrangle with the indignity of an imperialist, glorified diner in our country? And why do those poor people have to give you perfume in the toilet? This does not make me feel jauntily privileged. Such an act merely serves as a poignant reminder that capitalism has gone horribly wrong. Some poor sod is affixed to a stool for forty hours each week lulled into terrible complacency by the burbles, flushes and grunts of a hamburger-gulping, poorly dressed constituency. I blame Demi Moore. How does she sleep, particularly knowing that she could have had Robert Redford rather than Woody Harrelson. Will I spend my life with the director of the prestigious Sundance film festival who, despite the ravages of time, remains puppishly good looking or will I bonk the artless, idiotic bartender from *Cheers*? Some people do not deserve their good fortune.

2. The Liberal Party. It is glaringly obvious, I suppose, that I am a soft-left apologist. So you can choose to ignore this one if you prefer. Beyond their offensive policies and teeming disregard for social justice, however, they really are just a pack of thick-as-shit losers. At the very least, the ALP knows how to get pissed loudly in a Chinese restaurant. The Libs remain, despite their flaccid protestations, a bunch of private-school wankers who love rugby union and really bad novelists like Ayn Rand. Further, they can't hold their piss. They think a rank and file is something that dirty union delegates use when they're on the shop floor; they like ladies to wear hats indoors and they're no fun at parties. And what's this shit about not saying sorry to indigenous Australians? We are all implicated in our nation's history. I, like a lot of average sucks, am fascinated by my family tree. I want to be proud of my genealogy, but I also want to learn from my ancestors' mistakes. The refusal to apologise politely is the shittiest kind of untoward, blind, compulsive atavism imaginable. One could be forgiven for thinking that Robert Menzies remains alive and well.

3. Alcoholic Soft Drinks. What's wrong with a lager? Of course, a frivolous traditional cocktail is acceptable on occasion. However, for the most part there should be a certain amount of pain involved in any alcohol consumption. I want to know that I'm drinking, damnit. I resent the implicit suggestion in Sub Zero's niche marketing that I am not womanful enough to drain a schooner glass. Haven't the compact inner-city darlings who so vehemently embrace this foul pus realised yet that they're sucking on an immediate relative of the wine cooler? Further, despite what clinicians might say about there only being one kind of alcoholic inebriation, this abhorrent lemonade produces a very flighty drunk. Give me the staccato, fractured demands of a vodka drinker! The mawkish love of my comrades well bloated

by beer! The plump proselytising of one who is giddy with haute medoc, the dark insights of a bourbon lover or even the prim pronouncements of an unwooded chardonnay victim are all preferable to the sticky effervescence of some dickhead who's had ten DNAs.

4. Certain Media Moguls. Kerry Packer is the major shareholder for Channel Nine. These are the people who give you *Australia's Funniest Home Video Show*, Hey! Hey! It's Bollocks and Ray. This profligate crime hardly bears the weight of any substantial analysis. Beyond the immanent and monumental cruelty, snide homophobia and plain crushing lies proffered by these and other locally produced programs, what is it with the Channel Nine Chicks? Teutonically blonde, saucer-eyed and supremely, sunnily fucking stupid ... I wonder what Ros Packer thinks of these women? Really, though, Kerry can only boast five billion dollars worth of assets. More of a duchy than an empire. Bill Gates is infinitely wealthier so, it would follow, proportionately more despicable. Like many, however, I reluctantly admire his savvy in buying the rights to DOS for about three bucks. And even though I'm one of the few Mac-heads left in digital Christendom, I really like that new red squiggly line spellchecker that appeared in Word 6. One is compelled, drawing upon the dual preconditions of idiocy and lavish wealth, to abominate Rupert Murdoch the most. Two words: Super League. What was he thinking? Detonating his shiny parcel of avarice right in the middle of orthodox club culture. Bastard. Then there's all the pompous ultraright shit in his tawdry newspapers, his reels of crappy coaxial cable and his general plans to purchase the cosmos.

5. Gourmet Pizza. As someone who was, doubtless, modestly sagacious once said: don't fix it if it ain't broke. Patently, the pizza form does invite a modicum of experimentation.

Admittedly, under the influence of beer, fatigue and desperate hunger, I have bashfully participated in the construction of a tuna-in-brine, instant whip potato and macadamia-nut shambles. I learnt my hard culinary lesson, however, and now keep only a cautious selection of customary pizza toppings on hand. The same cannot be said for the evil vendors of goat's cheese, apple and venison travesties. They have been at it for at least a decade, these infidels, their toweringly maladjusted imaginations providing the only apparent limit to their heinous pizza crimes. And dessert pizza! What is that supposed to achieve, precisely? The finely calibrated marvel that is Italian cuisine provides manifold delicious alternatives to this sucrose travesty. Tiramisu, gelato, cassata and biscotti are all delicious, time-honoured classics that remit absolutely no degree of embarrassment or nausea to the devourer. On occasion, I am resoundingly shocked by the human monster's capacity for evil.

6. Inordinately Wet, Perfervid And Supportive Teachers. In the inaugural year of my resoundingly unsuccessful academic lurk, I acceded to passionate hatred for certain of my traditional modernist philosophy tutors. At least since the time of Socrates, pedagogical love has been a prerequisite for passing Classical Systems of Thought 101—except I guess it wouldn't have been called classical back then. Doubtless, in the Hellenic gymnasiums of old, one would have to bear frothy pep-talks, empathy and camaraderie in exchange for a tiny bit of epistemological insight. Just as Plato wouldn't have told you about the four forms unless you agreed to have a beer with him at the union bar after class, contemporary wankers persist in boring you senseless with their narratives on Sartre and How His Concept Of Being For Others Relates To The Embarrassingly Inert State Of My Sex Life. In any case, philosophy teachers often suck, and so do their artless, eager

admirers who lurch uncontrollably toward the front of the class screaming, 'Oh, yes, Heath! You're just so adorably right.' Mercifully, it is only a proportionately small number of citizens who swoon respectfully to the epicedium of bile that tumbles from the mean lips of fat little clever shits with Mars Bar erections. Everyone else at my university was too stoned to remember, or too sensible to actually attempt, a 'higher learning'. But it is High-School teachers who are the real criminals in this case. Who amongst us has not briefly endured the torment of a literature, drama or visual arts denizen who demanded that you reveal your 'inner self'? Teachers that lend you decent books the librarian is too 'proper' to buy, get you extra time on Adobe After Effects or take you on excursions to the morgue should be treasured. However, intransigent, rapacious lame dipshits who want to give you massages, take you to see *Last Tango In Paris* or make you listen to their poetry are crap. Report them to the Teachers Federation and then burn their Charles Bukowski books.

7. Crafty people. Cunning is fine when distilled in moderation, but decoupage is a crime. Why do some bizarre types persist in their crusade to stencil, enamel and doily-ise the world? Frames made out of alfoil, glazed pinch-pots and tie-dye are all symptoms of a deeper ill. On those occasions when cash flow refused to coincide with holiday events, I have been known to distribute ungainly bits of cardboard with stringy-bark clagged to its edges. However, there are those who can afford to give a nice software package, a mohair blanket or some quality crockery and who elect instead to proffer a macramé owl. This is cute when you're seven and sweetly penniless but a mortal insult if you're thirty and in the high tax bracket.

8. Soggy cooking. In an age where hypermarkets ably purvey kaffir lime leaves, polenta and chum soy, the amateur

gourmand cannot continue to claim refuge in rissoles. I am a shit-house cook, but I do know the difference between a bunch of aragula and my arse. And what's with this unprincipled hectoring of virgin vegetables? Why do nascent domestic tormentors transform a regal, fibrous, tumescent and towering emerald vegetable like broccoli into a shirking grey pile of intestinally challenging, barely esculent coils of plain disaster? (Then proceed to limply adorn a 'gourmet' pizza with it?) Food is heaven and it troubles me that there are those who approach it with prosaic, utilitarian need.

9. Myself. I'm such a bitter, angry woman. Oh, my infancy was traumatic and I spent far too many vacuous hours sucking on objects unwholesomely pigmented with lead paint. Nobody understands me and, try as I might, I just can't spot reduce! I once publicly announced that 'Michael Hutchence has a lot of unwieldy bottle calling his new album *Elegantly Wasted*. This was a term cautiously coined to describe Keith Richard. Michael Hutchence bears the same resemblance to Keith Richard as my shopping list does to *J'accuse*.' And now he's dead, oh woe, and I'm to blame. I smoke cigarettes, imbibe cholesterol with the churlish ease of a Sun Bear, and my Stair Master lies in a dusty shroud of neglect. I hate myself. Are you kidding? If it is not already sufficiently evident, I've actually got corporate box-seat tickets on myself. If there is one thing that, to borrow the gaudy parlance of one of my colleagues, really gets up my clacker, it's modesty! Isn't it so much more artful to take yourself out on a metaphoric dinner date, spoil yourself coyly with flattery and to smugly know that you are drop-dead clever? Caress your undulating specificity, I say, and preferably with a daubing of high-potency vitamin E oil. Amaze and bore oscillating others with your chilling, unbroken litany of great achievement. Don't dash

your hope on the saw-toothed rocks of prim social protocol. Self-aggrandisement is not altogether alienating, deleterious to your goals or just plain repugnant. You can loudly love yourself sick WITHOUT coming across like some loony, latter-day Vanilla Ice. It's got to be said, chicks are decorated post-grads in the insipid faculty of You're So Much Better Than Me. Why are ladies so adept at corroding their own splendid cores with auto-derision? A seemingly circumspect abnegation of conceit might just land you in one or two supremely dysfunctional relationships. Ultimately, however, you will only reify your protestations of inadequacy. Amour-propre and heavy mettle are your only safe-guards in this murky universe against disaster. Don't ablate the vanity gland!

10. The hierarchy of celebrity. How often has your self-esteem been mitigated by the mere fact of your nonappearance AGAIN! in *Who Weekly*'s annual list of the universe's twenty-five most intriguing people? A fraught issue and one, I'm afraid, that demands an entire capacious chapter on its own. Read on!

CHAPTER FIVE

AIRPORT CLUB LOUNGES, MY LAMENTABLE PROPENSITY FOR JOINING THEM, & ALLEGED VIP STATUS IN GENERAL

As an electronic media celebutante of only minor notoriety, I perceive myself as oddly placed in this decade's peculiarly obsessive hierarchy of fame. At ambivalently 'glittering' events I provide, I concede, photo opportunities for only the most woeful, lethargic and misguided paparazzi stalkers. On the odd occasion that I do receive privileged treatment (NB: This usually takes the form of some retrograde laminated badge, gratis tepid flat beer and a limp handshake from someone only marginally more 'significant' than I), I find myself both excessively needy and humiliated. Why do so many of us flock forlornly to the penumbra of renown? Why do I spend needless dollars on Airport Club Lounge passes, only to discover that even within these rarefied sanctuaries, there are further, better, plusher rooms called Captain's Club intended for real sky-bound VIPs? I detest this inclination in myself and find it equally pernicious in others. We pursue contact with wealth, talent, beauty, privilege and influence as though they were viruses from which we might seek contagion and self-improvement. We are never sated in our quest for status.

We continue to suspect that there is a conspiracy frustrating our quest for comfort.

As documented previously and rigorously by solid thinkers, fame, and all its concomitant rewards, functions in our age as the undisputed canon of victory. To be unswervingly famous in the late twentieth century is to be consummately blessed. In commanding the focus of mass media attention on one's self, an individual wields the power and privilege once reserved for monarchs. Of course, occasionally the famous have to bear such indignities as having their cellulite highlighted in crappy women's magazines. However, the relatively minor discomfort of such thigh exposure merely restates the object's pre-eminence.

For every square centimetre of imperfect celebrity skin that is documented, there is a proportionate reward. Whether it is a revelation of orange-peel-esque adipose tissue, painkiller abuse or a failed marriage, such disclosure is ultimately beneficial to the star's marketability. While magazines and insubstantial television journalists persist in their baring dispatches, the notable does not run the risk of having his or her 'humanity' expunged. Rather, it is enhanced by this scrutiny. Folly not only makes great copy, its appearance convinces all us consuming idiots that the VIP in question is terribly brave and terribly human. They have succeeded against the odds! Hey, they're just like you and me, we think, erroneously.

We embrace celebrity inadequacies and we revere their tragedies. This has been vividly articulated in the schlock journo's overused quasi-homily: Death Is A Great Career Move. It is my opinion that Elvis was a bloated, racist shit with some very profound and unresolved Oedipal issues. He also recorded the noisome 'Teddy Bear' and gave jumpsuits a very bad name. We are all aware that Marilyn Monroe was merely a modestly gifted, immensely insecure comic actor with fabulous breasts and a penchant for prescription remedies. Further, Jim Morrison was a less writerly Lou Reed whose little snake hips looked great in leather pants. The schlong that he so loved to eulogise and swing about was markedly smaller than that of the infinitely cooler Iggy Pop, and his major shifting contribution to twentieth century art lay in setting the foundations for the seventies advent of radio friendly Adult Oriented Rock. (Frankly, I'm much more impressed by charismatic geniuses who proactively defy death. Despite his protestations that it was merely an exercise in 'lymphatic drainage' or some such, as a resolute early-to-mid period Stones fan I will forever mythologise Keith Richard's valiant attempt to have his blood changed at a Swiss spa.)

Currently, stars are actually wresting control of their own monies and now register private production companies. Justifiably jaded by the avarice of studio moguls, they now emerge as corporate citizens in their own right. Death, of course, would effectively delete the possibility of competent investment practice so, in order to preserve their lionised status, bigwigs just get as close to death as possible. Or, at the very least, their mental or physical health should be seriously, if judiciously, challenged to maintain fiscal buoyancy. Oprah's bilious and televised battle with her weight has proven a ratings winner. Would anyone really give shit about how well she interfaced with crossdressing bulimic crack babies if she didn't stack on fifty kilos every Sweeps Week? As employees of the star of *Kindergarten Cop* and other holiday blockbusters, Arnold Schwarzenegger's sagacious publicists chose not to jeopardise his suburban appeal by constructing his necessary Achilles heel around his youthful 'exploitation' at the hands of European pornographers. Fortunately, his rather public heart surgery saved him from Teutonic perfection. (Which is good, I suppose, cos I didn't want to see those sappy, faux-classical photographs of him and his little steroid penis again, thanks.) Tom Cruise is an avid scientologist who patently doesn't understand the technology of fame. He's so squeaky clean and seamless as to be endangered. When a German newspaper ran a story alleging that he was impotent, he should have dipped into his capacious L Ron Hubbard-inspired cash management account and paid them! Surely litigation wasn't a suitable response from a man in such desperate need of a problem. Our own Jason Donovan reacted with analogous imprudence when he sued British magazine *The Face* for photo-shopping him neatly into a 'Queer As Fuck' T-shirt. Jase had recently recorded 'Especially For You', so perhaps the only interesting thing about him at the time was his rumoured homosexuality. Crazy Jason has enacted an overt about-turn since his *Face*-slapping days, of course, and now persists in falling down ostentatiously in over-priced delis, wearing silly woollen hats and hanging out at the site of River Phoenix's messy death, the Viper Room. Poor Mr Donovan. If he was real estate rather than failed celebrity commodity, the classified ad would euphemistically read 'A Real Renovator's Delight!' No amount of precision public relations, homophilic attachment or drug abuse will save him.

(Perhaps I need to qualify some of my latter statements. Fear not. I still regard The Doors with suspicion and I'm not about to commence a campaign of sentiment on behalf of oppressed, formerly chubby talk-show hostesses. I mean to clarify my references to Jason's alleged 'perversion'. Homophobia, of course, is a virulent ill and had I not been so frequently and pitiably leftie throughout this text, I would have included this disease as an object of vehement scorn in the previous Crankiness Template. Disdain for my gay brothers and sisters in any form is unwarranted, myopic and crap. However, I do worry that Same Sex Love continues to function as a travesty or 'tragedy' in the symbolic order of celebrity. Perhaps this is something you need to discuss rigorously amongst yourselves. Yet I am compelled to wonder if, for example, Ellen Degeneres cynically assessed the market viability of her dual television/in-real-life Coming Out episode. Is Ellen an effective civil libertarian or is she simply commodifying the fact of her own lesbianism? Has she merely allowed her Sapphism to supplant the prerequisite celebrity 'problem'? Are we, as a stupendously thick and predictable audience, forced to opine: Oh, I can relate to her. I've got limited social skills, thin fly-away hair and a huge arse and she's a PERVERT! Talk amongst yourselves, kids. Here's the topic. Ellen Degeneres: Revolutionary or Reactionary? Just one other thing, though. Who didn't know she was a dyke in the first place? For those of us who actually hang out with gay folk, it was as 'unexpected' as kd, Elton or Martina coming out! Oh, so you're gay! Well, I never and knock me over with a closet door. Duh! Back to the plot.)

Any rambling about fame's potency and repugnance would not be complete without reference to Princess Diana. Yes, yes. Wonderful woman, charitable angel, tragic loss and oh! those poor boys. No, really. I mean, I'm not actually going to sit in front of CNN and enjoy the painful death of a sexy, seemingly altruistic young demi-activist and mother. It must be noted also that for a person of abbreviated education, she made a splendid conceptual leap in determining that her function as consciousness raising glamour-puss would benefit more people than choosing the orthodox, decorous, regal route of 'charity' work. She realised that it was important to fundamentally alter people's belief systems to ensure substantial change. She didn't just generate piddling amounts of money and expect applause, like Bob Geldof for instance. Anyway, Diana's good name and the politics of quick-fix, feel-good donations aside … let's get back to fame!

At the time of writing, no-one has yet decided how The Princess died. It may have been exuberant paparazzi scum or a rat-arsed drunk-driver. Whatever the actual cause, most folks seem to favour the former notion and, even if they don't, her death is still viewed as the logical, symbolic conclusion to a life lived under media scrutiny. Well, bullshit. It was simply a hideous accident and, unless you are a Great French Thinker Of The Modern Or Postmodern Period, you can't expect people to weave your death by vehicle into anything like a significant textual reading. By her own admission, Princess Diana aspired to be the 'Queen of People's Hearts'. Her relentless campaigning for justice only became meaningful under media surveillance. Unfortunately, it can't all be deferential Op Ed pieces in *The Times*, discreet profiles on *BBC World* and tasteful photo shoots in *Vanity Fair*. In our uncompromising world, you've gotta take the rough with the smooth, the shit with the shinola and the *New Idea* with the *New Yorker*. She was mates with Clive James, so I'm sure he must have warned her of something along these lines. In any case, these days Diana is shriven, lots of people are making money off commemorative Princess tea sets and the whole messy business has ratified the tantrums of more whining superstars.

We have discussed, have we not, eager students, the means by which one attains a protracted and sustainable celebrity. A chewy problem is the key. Diana herself was shot to mega-repute with the assistance of bulimia, divorce and depression. In a bizarre late-millennial twist, celebrity itself has now become a problem to problem-dependent celebrities. Didn't anyone tell them that media attention was in the job description? Does the querulous Demi Moore actually just expect to do her 'art' in a vacuum? I believe that there are very few people who wish to 'entertain'—or, conceivably, just very few people—who are bereft of the desire for mass admiration. (Possibly Thomas Pynchon, his mate JD Salinger or the very disinterested and broke looking female stripper I observed performing on stage at The Love Machine with her hot-magenta battery-operated device some weekends ago). For precisely what period of time these media protagonists can expect from us the empathy that maintains them is uncertain. I wonder if we will retain our imagined and con-genial rapport for very much longer. Personally, when I search for an analogue in my life to Madonna's cries of 'You're crushing me with your devotion!' I can find none. I loved and understood her when she declared her penchant for promiscuity. I embosomed her and transmitted concord when she displayed a touching fond-ness for cheap lingerie. When she copiously despised Kevin Costner, I cheered! And finally, even though I would never think of shagging either Sean Penn or Warren Beatty, I deluded myself that she was just like me. The corollary of all of this was that I shelled out thirty bucks and bought *The Immaculate Collection*. Now that she shirks recognition, I won't even think of buying her albums. How can anyone expect me to believe that having people taking notice of you is bad?? Bugger off. I, like so many, abundantly crave regard. In darker contemplative moments aboard a commercial aircraft I have considered taking the emer-gency advice in using the whistle affixed to my lifejacket TO ATTRACT ATTENTION! Just blow, Ms Ciccone.

(On a, her hum, personal note, as a broadcaster, I get to talk with some of the famous nutters. A process I find strangely compelling! With few exceptions, I am regardful, polite and handy with a herbal tea bag. I thank them for their time and always provide a five-minute window in which they can bang on egotistically about the travails of being endlessly interviewed. Admittedly, some of my peers are utter fucks and reputedly give their famous guests a hard time. But that's really no excuse for being a total, unfaltering grump, and I'd say that a remarkable proportion of them are. Just to indicate my soft, feminine side, I should say that there are some really sensible famous folk I have encountered and these include kd lang, Pierce Brosnan, John Tesh, Jennifer Love Hewitt, Pat Rafter, Veruca Salt, Kim Beazley and, I haven't met him, but one of my mates tells me that Keith Richard is top!)

I have stated that this text is forged in a spirit of generosity. I have cast myself, as stated, in the valiant role of the anti-Deepak Chopra. I have aspired, in this chapter, to heighten your hate-awareness and to apply the mantra Everything's Fucked in a mass media context. And now, we must take action! Of course, the most obvious rebellion against luminaries who refuse to openly luxuriate in their fortune is to not see their movies, buy their CDs or visit their web sites. You could also get creative, I guess, and call ticketing agencies from public phones and then run away leaving the receiver engaged. Do this when Motley Crue next threatens to visit. Or maybe tell your little brother that Sporty Spice is actually a man and he'll spread it around school at speed. The best and last line of defence against the contemporary cult of noxious, ignoble celebrity is, of course, to become famous yourself. Please begin practising my suggestions forthwith!

HELEN'S NEVER FAIL FIVE POINT PLAN
FOR IMBUING THE WORLD WITH YOUR FABULOUS IMAGE
1

Begin to contextualise your current mode of life. Think of your present in a media milieu as it will eventually become your Dark Troubled Past. Are you doing something faintly illegal or unhealthy? If not, begin posthaste. When you select your mode of bad behaviour, make it enduring and classic. It could be some time before you're on *Larry King Live*, so consider the shelf life of your misbehaviour options carefully. In the modern framework, hacking or phone-phreaking might seem the very essence of modern miscreant style. However, they'll probably be (a) passé or (b) punishable by death at the hands of the Microsoft Corporation by the time you get to talk about them on the telly. Unwavering drug addiction, while it seems to persist as a popular celebrity wile, can basically preclude the possibility of you ever doing anything useful or attention-worthy ever again. Feigning a substance abuse problem may prove a desirable alternative to actually having one. Go to the toilet a lot, hurl phantom rats out your car window à la Robert Downey Junior and hang around hock shops. Just *pretend* to be fucked up.

2

Learn three chords on the guitar, rent a *You Can Act!* video or marry one of the Friends. Even if it is simply the Hollywood-approved practice of Upward Dating, your special skill must be honed. Become a talent miscellanist until you find something tenable and only minimally humiliating. When you have something to boast about and market, go to lots of silly parties even if they don't let you in at first. Design and place a web site and run around to a lot of terminals at public libraries hitting your page. Importantly, never doubt your ability to emerge as one of the decade's Brightest Young Stars. Hell, if Rob Lowe managed to stride through the eighties like a god, a single cell organism probably can in these de-evolutionary times. Buy some aqua-marine contact lenses, employ a Super-Agent and leak a compromising home video of yourself to the press.

3

Avoid the Viper Room or anywhere else that you might find Jason Donovan. And remember, by the time a venue or bar is publicly enshrined as 'in' it is resolutely 'out'. Choose rarely visited, tacky dung-holes above attested winners. If you are steadfast in your presence at a particular establishment, you may begin to notice the clientele transform. Just purr around looking hip and many misguided fools will follow. Oh, don't try this at Sizzler. It just won't work.

4

Pretend to be really interested in the press when they start sniffing around you. Sympathise with their plight and say things like 'Despite the burden this places on my sense of self, I really appreciate what you guys are doing for me. Did you see my profile in *Interview* magazine? Hell, your writing is SO much richer and far less prolix.' A little sycophancy goes a long way.

5

When you are famous, use Dean Martin as a template and not Demi Moore! Be an incorrigible fame volupte and roll around hoggishly in your wall-to-wall privilege. Wear silk pyjamas, buy a gaudy mansion and have flagrant (safe latex-bound) sex romps on the shag pile. Make other famous friends, have lots of lovely surgery and, hey, send me some photos! Why do some notorious imbeciles pretend not to enjoy their influence, Swiss bank accounts and antique car collections? And as for disdaining the untoward attentions of the press … well, I used to get excited when the Kodak representative visited my seat of learning for school photo day! Lap up *any* attention!

If, somehow, you remain resolutely timid and this plan fails, there are other therapies available. The next chapter addresses moments in which you are entitled, NAY COMPELLED!, to behave like a very bad person.

CHAPTER SIX

NAUGHTINESS WITH IMPUNITY

Here we will discuss when and why it is socially sanctioned for you to have a tantrum. We will revisit and expand upon bad behaviour and begin with a deeply personal account of my own doughty Teen Envy. We will examine the possibility for stout relentless pleasure and revolution in the new classification of codified kiddiness. Finally, for those amongst you who have surrendered to the ancient denaturation of maturity, I will offer a salve in the form of my now famous Never Fail Five Point Plan.

'I AM AN ADULT!' I insist to myself at doubting intervals. I teeter wretchedly on the precipice of thirty. I hold, at last survey, no less than five credit and/or charge cards in my fawn-leather faux-Italian wallet. I have a subscription to *Vanity Fair*, I'm thinking about starting a collection of Dutch colonial curios circa 1880, and in February I starved for three months and secured my first sombre sub-designer female suit. (Well, I did make that purchase on the sage advice of my solicitor who was defending me on criminal charges. But that's barely relevant. I still look very urban in it.) In any case, I possess the paraphernalia of a moderately successful mature reality, and not all of it is on hire-purchase. If you met me at a dinner party you'd probably concede, at first, that I am, in fact, one of the grown-ups. Then WHACK! your sensible brain would produce some synaptic marginal gloss like, 'Who's the loud blonde pretending to know all about Penfolds' best vintages and the history of the Mabo decision? Hope she doesn't vomit in the pot plant when she finally shuts up.' And the game would be up. Okay then, I'm a putative pubescent.

To be just, one cannot merely attribute my unswerving immaturity to some neural glitch and/or developmental obstruction. I believe fervently that my lack of substantial socio-cultural growth can be posited in a broader and systematised context. My refusal to act like anything other than an eighteen year old is not my fault! Like any defiant, spotty teenager, I blame society. (And I reckon Channel Nine's got a lot to do with it too. We'll explore that shortly.)

Like so many of my peers, I am burdened with Protracted Adolescence Disorder. Progenitors beware! This dysfunction, publicly evinced by such luminaries as Bill Gates, Jerry Seinfeld and Courtney Love, is virulent and may be financially perilous. Malapert owners of factory-fresh newborns may naively expect to extricate themselves from toxic parental bondage in, perhaps, twenty years. PAD ensures, beyond doubt, that in the year 2029 you'll have a whining, procrastinating, shop soiled thirty-one year old sill begging you for money and leaving their (Mambo) clothes on the bathroom floor. Sadly, there is little, at this juncture in history, that can be done. As an unwilling sufferer I urge you to support me in my quest to devise a cure. I propose to begin a new and vigilant epidemiology! And so, let us examine the origin, the technology and the symptoms of this noisome ill. For, through understanding we may learn to curb it.

Naturally, PAD would not exist had adolescence itself never been reified. The 'teenager' is, of course, a concept that began as a commercial fiction and later mutated into a contained disease. Do not assume for a deluded nano-second that the state of being 'teenage' is somehow anterior to electronic mass media! Television demands and forges niche markets. It doesn't respond to them. (To illustrate: the cathode poison of *Hey! Hey! It's Saturday* does not answer an essential biological hunger for detritus. In a Rousseauian 'state of nature', I believe, we humans would be naturally inclined toward Franz Kafka, *Absolutely Fabulous* and other flawless entertainments. Channel Nine has just been covertly making us, over the last four decades, stupid enough to tolerate a wheezing cynic like Red Symons.)

Having established that adolescence was invented half a century ago (possibly by the CIA) to provide an eager audience for such pointless rubbish as 'See You Later, Alligator', we now turn our attention to the seventies. The constituents of the 'teen-age' phenomenon were forced to look on as their elders fuddled about with middlebrow modalities such as Jungian psycho-analysis, Pink Floyd and, HORROR, the notion of the 'inner child'. This latter unctuous adjunct to late twentieth century pop therapy compounded the petri-platter of pubescence and provided the foundation for the PAD we now confront. Youth, or the state of flux—or 'Becoming' as French philosopher Deleuze would have it—became a heterodox religion! And so now you understand why I, an ABC employee, have a collage of Skeet Ulrich pictures around my Mac monitor. And perhaps why a thirtyish comrade, employed as a legal aid solicitor (an LlB and BEc [hons]), wears Converse sneakers to court, writes poems about Keanu and stood in line for five hours to get tickets to the Prodigy.

As indicated previously, fortysomething Jerry Seinfeld is a

poster-child for PAD. He and his contemptible sitcom friends display no adult virtues, work is secondary to their predilection for breakfast cereal, and their intimate relationships are disposed of via ansafone contretemps. At the very least, however, Seinfeld provides an implicit literate critique of the malaise I have called PAD. The infinitely more popular *Friends* merely celebrates it without question. At the time of writing, Jennifer Anniston ('Rachel') is widely regarded as one of the most desirable women in America! She loves to shop, wear cute clothes and partake in sweaty congress with the pusillanimous David Schwimmer in public places. Isn't she supposed to be twenty-eight?

Evidence of PAD is everywhere you turn. Brokers buy in-line skates, snowboarding hats and copies of the *Anarchist's Cookbook* in Brunswick Street. Thirty-five year old personal assistants in Sydney subvert their corporate firewalls and congregate at the Yahoo chat site Chick's Who Wanna Hurt My Penis. Twentysomething failed arts students speak to a national audience of millions every afternoon about quality toilets, *Party Of Five* and rilly rilly cool web sites. (Three to six weekdays on Triple J. Don't miss it!) What's wrong?

The towering inability to evolve encroaches. 'Profession' is itself becoming an outlandishly unfashionable ideal. Increasingly one's integrity is measured in terms of the ability to name all of the All Saints without hesitation. Former articles in the compendium of conspicuous mature success such as European luxury cars, Penguin classics and a 'trophy' mate are being rapidly supplanted by such totems as skateboards, an alphabetised mint condition Manga collection and a fabulously disastrous, distinctly unhealthy quasi-relationship where more time is spent conferring hotly as to which partner has been playing Doom the longest, rather than actually performing moist, tender acts of physical love. The corporate boardroom of an effortlessly teenage tomorrow will be entirely staffed by pierced, Hot Tuna clad and Chupa-Chup imbibing infidels who employ the term 'filth' with the lexical prowess, passion and verity of an eight year old who has been chemically transmutated by red cordial and wind. In this new economy, Rene Rivkin's home fax number has infinitely less currency than the prowess to procure backstage passes for a Marilyn Manson gig. (It will all come down to the size of your steeple!) We are always, as indicated previously, Becoming rather than Being.

Adulthood, I believe, may be viewed as a 'modern' state. Modernity, beginning with the Enlightenment, is characterised by notions such as Progress, Serious Certainty and Literal Facts. Postmodernity, by contrast, apotheosises Deconstruction, Playful Doubt and Figurative Fiction. If heavyweight French thinkers are to be believed, grown-ups, as we know them, will shortly be devoured by the yawning postmodern impasse. So, you see, it might be okay for me to keep painting my fingernails black, interviewing pop stars and asking my mum to do my tax. Jacques Derrida demands it!

Well, Jacques doesn't have a problem with it, neither do I and, no doubt, if he had not been unconditionally squashed by a Parisian laundry truck in an instant of pure existential cruelty, nor would Roland Barthes. For individuals as bemused by, inimical to and pissed off with the orthodox technologies of society, discourse and self as I, PAD is great news. I suggest that you begin to use it to your best advantage at once. Now that the potential for human caprice, flux and pointless amelioration has been extruded from the hitherto mean lower colon of the western world, the average dissatisfied boy or girl can take a swipe at approved action.

Nurturing the ill-washed and petulant teenager within is a vital exercise. As indicated, To Become rather than To Be is to outrun the elaborate delusion of reality. In pursuing childish, perpetually 'developmental' whims, one approaches the deconstructionist future. The simple pubescent act of not knowing what you want constitutes the commencement of a major philosophical shift. In refusing to always make your bed, you practicably near the viscose, irresolute conceptual template of the future. You don't want to be left behind for the new millennium do you, still wistfully clinging to your antique schematisation where 'rational' dichotomous thought, unified 'individuality' and the 'representational' nature of speech and text limply preside? No! You want to be a teleological terrorist to whom nothing is true, knowable or immutable. I mean, when the *New Weekly* starts running articles on Hollywood And The Postmodern Impasse, where will you be? Sharon Stone will be renouncing her unified identity and changing her name to 'The' and, in the spirit of the new post-structuralist potlatch, offer a simultaneous re-enactment of her own experiences as an alleged hysteric analysand in neo-Lacanian psychoanalysis with *Basic Instinct* available only on pianola roll format, in hieroglyphics and DVD ROM. Bruce Willis will 'ambivalently consist' ('star' is, by then, an outmoded concept) in an interactive drama where he valiantly attempts to unpick the unsavoury and interdependent ideas of (a) the static symbolic order and (b) gender, by remaking the *Die Hard* series using only his penis. Oh, yes! A glorious day indeed it will be when nearly all luminaries enact deconstruction and actively seek to exploit the gaps in all things. Unfortunately, Elle Macpherson won't really get it. She will merely employ the faux-postmodern axiom she had rehearsed years earlier—'I don't read anything I haven't written myself'—and then she'll release a new line of undergarments with

Hip Derridean Holes in the crotch. Further, philosophy will become the new pornography, synaesthetes will emerge as the new couturiers, and McDonald's will offer free hermeneutics tutorials to anyone who can eulogise the ingredients of the now extant Big Mac in the form of multilingual performance poetry while sitting naked daubed only by special sauce in the doughy confines of a sesame seed bun. *Melrose Place* will become a housing cooperative populated exclusively by transgender lyricists who employ plastic surgery solely as a means to destabilise the nearly outmoded delimitations of morphology; Madonna will enter her most commercially successful period to date known simply as the 'Not Phase' while she does not perform, appear, design, ratify or indeed have any allegiance at all to her new video *Immaterial Girl* and, well, what with everything else erupting and oozing and refusing the stricture of a final authority, no-one will pay any attention to Michael Jackson. In the interim era, people will drop tabs of acid only to seek respite and relative logic from a world that has become altogether too trippy. Shopping lists will bear the weight of textual analysis and comparative reading. The members of Devo will be recalled and revered as the bearers of great polysemic prescience. No-one will believe in no-one. God will die. The act of incarceration will be applauded as the new comedy. Naturalistic drama will be regarded with suspicion and realistic fiction will become a punishable offence. This is your future. Embrace it!

Any old how, in my new capacity as the gloomy Faith Popcorn of post-Foucauldian malaise (yeah, right), I estimate that we now have a couple of months to prepare for the inevitable flummery of core meaninglessness. You don't have to start performing your own metaphoric reconstructive surgery just at this moment. However, I sternly advise that you prepare for the new impossibly fluid epoch and begin following my surly, childish example. It's the only logical and historically circumspect thing to do! We've been getting immature for a while now. We will continue to de-evolve into an undifferentiated infantile state. This may be observed chronologically. Before the Enlightenment, men (sic; chicks were only doorstops back then) acted as gods, prophesying and soothsaying, believing Plato and generally hurling great thunderbolts of truth around like there was no earthly tomorrow. After the Enlightenment, folks were content merely to function as messengers of God, strutting around proving that He existed. The industrial era or thereabouts breathed life into your basic Rational Thinker and social theorist. These zealous men and women were sort of missionaries-cum-schoolteachers who knew what was proper and threatened a spanking to those who did not concur. The modern period gave birth to the doubting adult who revelled, to some extent, in his or her own uncertainty and marvellously rich texture. (It also gave birth to Ernest Hemingway. Eugh.) We have now drifted to the furthest point away from absolute faith in our omnipotence. We are metamorphosing into teenagers!

As copious estrangement, hostility and other Hate Management applications have not yet been superseded by either postmodern revolutionaries or a new Microsoft operating system, we must respect and adhere to these still relevant standards. Remember, at this juncture in history, nearly everything's fucked and involute animosity is the key! No other variety of western human knows combativeness, alienation and splenetic revolt like a teenager! As such, and as your indistinct saviour, I urge you to run off to your room in a huff during dinner, listen to the forlornly self-obsessed Smashing Pumpkins because, really, Billy 'Rat In A Cage' Corgan is the only man who'll ever understand you, and then, after sobbing implacably all night, miss your lift to school. Here, I offer another of my extravagantly researched paradigms for self-awareness and change.

HELEN'S NEVER FAIL FIVE POINT PLAN
FOR DEPOSING OBSOLETE MATURITY AND ACTING CUTE IN TIME FOR
THE POSTMODERN REVOLUTION

1

Accessorise. As a ruthless, relentless but reluctant consumer, the acquisition of material objects is my version of the wet New Age practice of 'affirmation'. Instead of saying 'I Am A Tower Of Strength Within And Without, Oh Gaia, Infuse Me With Your Verdant Earth Juice' and hoping woefully that you'll feel marginally better, I would recommend buying stuff. Who needs the western European goddess tradition and a pile of suggestive cassettes when there's shops like Neiman Marcus in the world? Sorry, I'm not truly being a total bourgeois hypermall empress. What I actually intend to convey is: if in difficulty, procure symbolic paraphernalia and your behaviour will change. Buy the signifier on credit card and the signified will arrive in thirty days. This is similar to my father's inspired but ultimately doomed insistence that my dexterity as a wicket keeper would improve if he first purchased the requisite cricket armoury for me. Pitiably enough, however, the closest I ever came to catching anyone out was seeing Mirabelle my PE teacher humming Joan Armatrading and holding hands with another hale, buckish lady after school one afternoon. There are some inalienable truths in the world and that I have no discernible facility for sports is one of them. Do not be deterred, however, by my limp, warm salad days' disappointment. Vigilantly pursue an emblem and trust that it can eventually and legitimately betoken the skill for which you yearn. And so the aspirant adolescent must stubbornly compile a garland of teeny-pie refuse. When adorning yourself, aim for the baubles of mid to late pubescence. The demi-teenager is too indistinct in his or her revulsion and not quite disturbed enough for our purposes. Further, it would be impractical of me to expect that any of you could motivate yourselves to publicly purchase Hanson's Christmas album. In any case, we wish to emulate and, finally, to definitively live the artless, naive cynicism of the sixteen year old. Clutch the evanescent whiner within and treat it to endless web browsing, compulsive if fickle attachments to moody Over-Wankers in the Eddie Vedder mould and, perhaps, a self-imposed allowance. Unfortunately, dark, oppressive parental forces tend to retire, pursue yogic workshops and take up residence on a Gold Coast canal development. Fortunately, one can analogise with relative ease between the Department of Social Security if one is an unemployed person, a wet perfervid schoolteacher (see previous chapter) if one is a student, or a repugnant manager if one is a paid worker. If you have marshalled the technology of hate as advised earlier, locating a punitive spoilsport to loathe in your life is uncomplicated. If you have a degree of difficult intimacy with any of these potential harassers, perhaps you could ask them to belittle you, not let you out on a Friday night and generally disapprove of your more intriguing friends. Rub your hands with gumleaves and eat two boxes of Tic Tacs on your way home from the pub to avoid smoke and alcohol detection. Miss the last bus. Set yourself a curfew and religiously break it. Become compulsively defensive when some dotard challenges the veracity of your passions. Say 'I do SO want to marry Pat Rafter!' Maintain a profoundly embarrassing dream journal for teen authenticity rather than actual 'self-discovery' (see passages on despising the New Age's wrong-headed insistence on the fact of knowable and contained selfhood). If you have started dressing like an adult, it may be problematic for you to return to lurid baby fashions. Personally, I have never redressed my habit of shopping in teeny aimed boutiques. Other women my age snarl at me and hiss 'mutton dressed as lamb' I am sure, but I know, ridiculous as I am, that it's for my own good. Accessorise! And accessorise with youthful ebullience, rather than aplomb.

2

Emote. Become vexatious, demonstrative and prone to tears. Enervated by real physical age, your hormones may now lope around your thirtyesque body with all the frenetic industry of a rusted Datsun 180B with two flats and a trailer full of old furniture affixed to a crumbling tow bar, but that's no adequate excuse. When confronted with an opportunity to aggressively opine, discredit, turn purple, avow love, harrumph, exit grandly or weep, seize it! Those in your immediate sphere of influence should be made aware exactly, if not overtly, of the torrid, teeming forces that govern the misshapen continent of your identity. Allow delicacy, bathos and goo to loudly conduct your behaviour in all affairs. Let the people know how you feel! Allow none of your torment to remain extrinsic to those that surround you. Remember: it's their problem too! And it's your job to boil, emote and theatricalise volitionally. Only today (I assert with the ardent, breathless punctilio of the self-help instructors from whom I have appropriated my inspiration and idiom) you have missed opportunities to breathe the foul stinking mist of your viscera in somebody else's face. Do you want to be an unwavering youngster? Begin immediately to overreact. If some abhorrent relative, for example, gropes absently in their handbag of Nanna Proverbs for something to impart and fetches that old familial standard, 'My, you've put on a little weight', do not let this window remain unsplintered. Create a great, walloping and dangerous fissure by screaming, roughly borrowing your argument from such endearingly wretched pop psychological tomes as *Fat Is A Feminist Issue* remembering to include references to Princess Diana's bulimia and then chug like an enraged diesel engine darkly out the door. Has an untoward colleague needlessly questioned your computer skills lately? This happens to me all the time. Engage them sternly if this is the case, allow your lower lip to tremble portentously and, before bursting into a monsoon of intractable moistness, admonish them extravagantly. Appear to valiantly hoist yourself from the muddied flats of despair and accuse your torturer thusly: 'Well (stifled sob!) I've actually been going through a really rough time, thanks, and your vengeful power mongering is not what I need right now'; refer, as suggested above, to Princess Diana's bulimia (it's particularly shrewd to usurp the dysfunction of this most immutably saintly figure) or some other malady and then, in a final purposeful evocation of the Everything's Fucked etiology, refer to the Crankiness Template and disyoke a stampede of hoary bile. 'Not only have you enacted a serious, punishable and distasteful transgression of orthodox workplace decorum in asserting your unasked for authority over my flawlessly performed duties, not only have you HURT ME, YOU BASTARD!' ultimately, you have furnished my long-held assumption that you are a digital fetishist who spends all available hours downloading unctuous horsey porn, acquiring the persona of somebody partially human in wet little romance sites and generally reconfiguring your hard disk in a compulsive, defensive manner in order to stave off the inevitable truth that nobody likes you and you're plain.' That kind of thing. Finally, if somebody has the audacity to dump you while you still determine a need for regular and unimpeded sweaty congress in your life, resort to the usual: ringing at 3 a.m. and then hanging up, having Pay Upon Delivery truck-loads of dirt delivered to the scrotum's domicile and assiduously placing silverfish amongst his/her prized robes. Emote! Emote with the flashy, histrionic, healthy vigour of a high-school student and not with the dull, careful, multilayered, convolute malaise of a grown-up.

3

Destroy. Or, at the very least, wilfully refuse to construct anything at all. Remember, you're a truculent teenager now and a manner of irresolute flux should inform your every gesture. Adolescence is often negatively perceived as being characterised by recalcitrance. It is viewed as a transient epoch in the arc of an individual's life where furious conceptual groping, deconstruction and the habit of problematising everything is prevalent. Such impressive, energetic practices should be affirmed rather than construed as fruitless and puerile. As such, you should pursue all activity in the spirit of the curious, fervid teenage electronics hobbyist to whom regular exploration of motherboards, clock radios and train sets is essential. You must now lasciviously desire first hand empirical knowledge of every device! The quest for an intricate, insatiable and intimate knowledge of the mechanics of just about everything—coffee makers, the construction of self, Channel Nine—is what sustains you. You are forced to ask, in turn: why Drip Filter technology? Why should I regard myself and others as unified vessels to whom any significant exchange of 'essence' is precluded? Why Red Symons, Ray Martin and Daryl Somers??? The very same indomitable verve that drove you to such heuristic, peregrine excursions like joining the International Socialists, cooking with lentils and donning midriff baring clothes should be revivified. This new mode may be enacted in simple, practical ways at first. To illustrate: acquiring a new 'interest', as cloyingly Christian and princey as this may initially appear, can liberate the flow of your smug adult synapses. I am personally never the bearer of more poison and jaded certitude than when I am learning a new skill or wrestling with strange and novel knowledges. As I have advised in other media, it's cool to swing! Golf is a scabrous, powerful reminder that you've got a shit-load left to learn. It is not uncommon for me to enjoy a postmodern epiphany as I tee off for the umpteenth time with a three iron while wondering haplessly if I'll ever be capable of efficiently wielding a wood. (Unhappily, the so-called 'fair' ways of our confused nation are frequently ruled by sexist, racist, triple-fronted brick-veneer weasels in amusing clobber. If you are of age, I recommend a bolt of pre-flasked and cautiously chilled lemon-infused Russian vodka at the third hole and several prudent indulgences thereafter to provide the necessary ballast against the clubhouse impropriety, slings and bloated boastfulness of others.) Further, challenging yourself to the nightmare episode in Quake, learning to recite irregular verbs in any language that is not your own, or embarking upon an agrobiological adventure with bonsai all constitute potential paths to anti-adult edification. None of these advances toward 'culture' are proffered in an attempt to engage you, dear, crazy reader, in a course of orthodox self-improvement. Rather, they are suggested in an effort to thoroughly destabilise you. Although neurological wizards and behaviourist types bang on darkly about the formative years as those that resolutely mould the individual, I believe that you can maintain your self-doubt, introspection and capacity for great disorder far beyond high school! Never believe the fiction that the stuff of which you are comprised is inexorable, irreducible or fated. You truly are endlessly equivocating Silly Putty. In personally defying the template of static organised selfhood, you also threaten to undermine the order of all things. Considering that we inhabit a fey fractious world that pollutes itself relentlessly with such solecistic chaff as greenhouse gas emissions, spandex and *Hey! Hey! It's Saturday*, it's only fair that we'd want to mess things up a bit. Of course, I am not saying, Nietzsche forbid, that We Are All In Control Of Our Own Destiny. We are, however, capable to an unattested extent of doing and thinking new things. We are equally adept at disposing of and unravelling the old things. Destroy! Destroy with the unfettered, itinerant and potentially reconstructive ease of the inquisitive junior, and do not accept the absurd and sluggish delusional certainty of the adult.

4

Masturbate. Pre-Kinsey, the act of—her hum—self-affrication was regarded with disdain and suspicion. Children were instructed to lie with their hands safely in view above the bedclothes lest they fall prey to enacting a spell of Satan's Embroidery. We have all heard the quaint and antique admonishments: it's not natural, it will impair your vision and, inexplicably, your evil secretions will fertilise your palms and cause them to sprout luxuriant hair. (Well, personally, I esteem little that consists in human industry as 'natural', I was born short-sighted and the palms of my hands are one of the very few of my bodily surfaces that does not require diligent depilation. And I've done my fair share of Olympic Standard Endurance Fiddling.) In any case, self-embrace was long disparaged as the relish of the obscene, the maladjusted and perverse. (Pre-eminent Nabakovian sicko Woody Allen probably didn't do much for wanking's good name when he pleaded 'Don't knock my hobbies!' But that's beside the point.) Walloping the rod, or strumming the flesh mandolin, is no longer scorned as an act of extreme effrontery and naughtiness. Nor is it, however, yet valued (beyond the parameters of questionable videos made in Canberra back sheds) as an acceptable and robust pastime. Post-Kinsey, autoeroticism shifted in the public perception from being perverse to being simply pathetic. Whacking off became something that sad people who couldn't get 'real' sex did in their mean little bedsits on substandard manchester. Or, significantly for our playful purposes, tossing was legitimised only if the potential tosser happened to be a callow urchin. As with so many purportedly 'perverse' or 'fetishistic' lascivious practices, wanking acquired the dubious status of a Phase in Human Sexual Development. (Don't misread me. Indubitably, there are some sexual acts that must be viewed as intrinsically wrong and nasty. Broadly, such acts are those which negate consensuality. I do not intend to transform into some slap-happy, ideologically mouldering hippie. I have never acknowledged the Do What You Wanna Do Be What You Wanna Be Yeah credo as tenable. Further, I bear an almost pathological disdain for the use of hessian in interior design.) By virtue of his or her frantic actions, the wanker is read as puerile or as one who has yet to competently nosedive into the pungent lagoon of adult sexual congress. In this schema, onanism is simply an hors d'ouvre, while missionary position heterosexual penetrative intercourse represents the main meal, the sorbet, the side salad, the dessert, the cheese plate and an assortment of sticky whites and exotic imported liqueurs. As previously discussed, this kind of linear, 'progressive' schematisation is fraught with danger and is responsible for our threshold axiom Nearly Everything's Fucked. Accordingly, with no regard for crockery, we must manfully and womanfully overturn the heaving tables of convention. Many of those things construed as negations must emerge for the new millennium as affirmations. Thus the term 'wanker' is no longer a slur but a statement of comfortable fact. And so, in pursuit of the ideals, machinery and techniques of adolescence, feel free to return to your unabashed game of crazy eights with mitigated shame, newly profuse brio and, possibly, an economy sized jar of some quality moisturising unguent. It is not that I subscribe, even for a deluded millisecond, to the hapless hebetude of 'swingers' who attend the promise of any sexual activity with the same awe as my Catholic ancestors may have done on the eve of a rare papal visit. Sexy stuff is not God nor Reason nor Defining Principle. It's just rather good, messy fun, as it happens. I am tireless in preaching the benefits of self-administered physical love, not because I actually care that profoundly about the sexual health of anyone with whom I do not exchange phone numbers, impassioned caresses and/or bodily fluids. In advising a jolly and effusive pull, I mean to tactically unwind the great fascistic chronograph of vermiform human maturation. You shouldn't just go about having apotropaic adult nooky so your friends think you're sophisticated. Revel in your developmental flaws and hail the usefulness of your most dexterous paw. Masturbate. Masturbate with the rakish, ebullient pride of a lusty pubescent and not with the burdensome, prickly coverture of a guilty grown-up.

5

Obsess. The trick here is not to become incorruptibly obsessive-compulsive or fixed in one's proclivities or habits. We can all, I conjecture, evoke the bedimmed contours of an ageing clansman or woman to whom routine and repetition have become essential.

The non-cubbish often impenitently fixate upon having dinner at precisely the same time each day, brushing their teeth each evening in an identical manner or throwing their tiny state-proffered stipend into the mean maw of exactly the same poker machine every pension day. Such obstinacy effects only a numbness and smugness of demeanour. It can also give you colon cancer. The most minor form of volition evaporates for the individual to whom even the purchase of an unexplored shoe polish is unthinkable. Such velleity is not our goal, modish readers. No! We desire, in the course of our lives, just about everything, with the possible exception of One Nation party membership. And we desire things variously. During a one-week period, for example, we may winsomely honour Ethan Hawke. (Ethan is posited here only for the sake of argument. Any person remotely involved with the lurid 'slacker' sham that was *Reality Bites* is probably not worthy of our attention. Wish I could have written the trailer for that rank, ulcerous piece of shit. He Was Armed With A Second-Hand Thesaurus And A Volume Of Hegelian Quotations. She Had Chronic Anorexia And A Closet Full Of Acetate Rayon Retro Dresses. Their Shared Putrescence, White Middle-Class Guilt And Lack Of Discernible Talent Brought Them Together. To paraphrase one of my preferred geniuses, Joe Queenan, why didn't they just eat Ethan when they had the chance in *Alive*?) Immediately following the Feast Of Ethan, we may select a suitable palliative to guard against the ghost of extreme lethargy and become, briefly, a Keanu habitue. (Now, I know Keanu's appeal is dwindling—interestingly, as he becomes less overtly teenage—but sometimes even Little Ms Postmodernity finds it hard to just let go. Further, who can forget the sterling musculature of his unhinged performance in *The Prince Of Pennsylvania*? Admittedly, scores of people do exactly this with ease if its constant availability at my local video store is any significant index. However, he is babe incarnate and will one day halt his credulous fiddling with strumpets like Amanda Who Is She Anyway De Cadenet and love me me me and only me.) Those with a taste for the ladies may easily employ this paradigm by simply replacing the names. Anyhow, parents are often heard to remonstrate their offspring with an endearing, 'I paid all this money for Ninjitsu classes and now you're just not interested in beating people up any more? Can't you stay interested in anything?' Well, no, frankly, we cannot. By consummating a marginal change in one's circumambience, these supposedly inconsistent teenagers may be praised for their liberal tastes rather than disdained for their perceived lack of endurance. It is better to know a little of everything than a lot of not much, n'est-ce pas? (My parents sent me to the Alliance Française. Sadly, I can only articulate French in the present tense and my vocab is abysmal, unless I'm chatting about Gallic dermatological preparations. Only useful if you want a facial, NOW! Buggered if I could make an appointment. However, I also have a rudimentary knowledge of reef knots from the Brownies. I've done a wine appreciation course and I know how to say 'barnyard' and 'big plums' in restaurants. I'm very chuffed about my ability to name all of the Ottoman sultans and at least two prominent Islamic architects. Further, I can also do a bit of digital video editing on my Mac, I have a rudimentary grasp of contemporary feminist French thought and I can vaguely play golf. Aaah, a life fully lived.) One must accomplish frequent transference. We must seize upon different objects of obsession. The Patriarchs of Psychoanalysis would, no doubt, see this as a symptom of neurosis. But, of course, until the revolution comes, we are all prisoners of desire, so it's best to share it around. Obsess. Obsess with the fluency, gorgeous caprice and planned obsolescence of a stylish youngster and not with the stoic, horrid immutability of an adult reactionary.

Accessorise. Emote. Destroy. Masturbate. Obsess. Done? Fine. Let's get back to hating unreconstructed, counterrevolutionary people and things.

CHAPTER SEVEN

WOMEN ARE FROM VENUS, APPARENTLY, AND I KNOW QUITE A LOT OF BLOKES WHO HANG OUT THERE, TOO

Here we will learn to enhance our ability to adamantly and efficiently taunt yet another invidious subsect of asinine losers. We will effectively acquire loathing for that bunch of cloddish 'thinkers' who presumptuously chronicle the supposed differences between men and women. There are those, oh genuinely gnostic readers, who industriously seek a return to a time when middle-class women were bound by the confines of formica and chintz and the average gent used Bryl-Creem without the liberal application of irony. As restated vehemently, human folks are capable of monumental morphing! The healthy citizen is not informed by a Wonder Bread past but is leaning instead toward infinite possibilities in infinite proportions (just like on *Star Trek —The Next Generation*). You will, doubtless, be soothed to know that the multigender Never Fail Five Point Plan is included at the end of this chapter for use by subjects who are socially defined as Woman and Man. And that probably means you!

Feminism's second greatest legacy after liberating women from assiduous depilation (not that there's anything intrinsically evil about hair removal, I just thank my valiant foremothers for disencumbering me of my shame in those weeks that I just can't seem to secure an appointment with the wax-woman) lies perhaps in forging the important metempirical distinction between gender and sex. This notional shift in perceiving beings as socially constructed and marked rather than as prisoners of a deterministic biology has transformed the western world irreversibly. Women no longer feel compelled to revere the 'sex is destiny' ethos and, congruously, pursue their need for subsidised day care, furnish themselves with the knowledge to ensure a socially equitable and personally prosperous future and, momentously, elegantly refrain from the purchase of appliqué kits in significant droves. Concurrently, perspicacious gentlemen callers invite their good and sports-fixated ladies to one-day matches with pride. These fearless but nonetheless mushy foot-soldiers of feminism embolden their strides to approach life as the competent carers of children and as the cooks of tasty baked dinners. These well-laundered men seek to thwart the sexual division of labour in the domestic realm. They may wait, if they are heterosexual, for up to three days after its initial release date to acquire the Swimsuit Issue of *Inside Sport*. Occasionally, these men, who are apprised of the wonder of Exit Mould, will agree to watch and legitimately enjoy *Fried Green Tomatoes At The Whistle Stop Cafe* or *Romy And Michele's High School Reunion* rather than *Die Harder* or *Back Door To Stuttgart* (A No Holds Un-Barred Deutsch Donger Fest Introducing Bavaria's Heidi Lavish-Torten And Johann Bratwurst Who Together Put Hitler's Beer Hall Putsch To Shame With Their Frothy Continental Antics!!). Happily, if incrementally, women and men are reifying feminism's phrenic goodness. We are changing. Then all these pointy little books pop up on the bestseller list in an effort to fuck it all up.

Hello? Simone de Beauvoir. Painstaking ethnographic research of different ways of being gendered humans. Equal pay. Female heads of state. Weren't you paying attention, John 'The Martian' Gray and your putatively caring, nurturing, regretful, loving drinking mates? More than likely, you were occupied writing and exchanging your own prescribed Love Letters.

Dear Rhonda,
1. I am angry that you fornicated with your Bridge Partner.
2. I am sad that you reckon she's a better root than me.
3. I am afraid that the blokes at my work are cacking themselves.
4. I am sorry that my organ is of such a modest size.
5. I love you and I wish that you'd come home from the women's housing cooperative.
Love, John.

The newly content and carnally satisfied Rhonda returns his letter.

Dear John,
1. I am angry that you keep writing me annoying letters.
2. I am sad that I left with you my forwarding address.
3. I am afraid that you've scratched my Tori Amos CD which, incidentally, I would like back.
4. I am sorry that you're such a dick.
5. You really shit me.
Piss off, Rhonda.

Actually, John Gray's sample Love Letters are infinitely more perverse than those above. They're much more prosaic and creepy. Kind of like:

Dear Poopsie,

1. I am angry that you used all my Redken phytology creme without asking me.
2. I am sad that there is no longer any air in my hair.
3. I am afraid that my locks will be keratin deficient and that you don't care.
4. I am sorry that you have not yet found a hair-care system appropriate to your need.
5. I love you and admire you for wanting to maintain your tonsorial health.

Love, Honey Bear.

PS. The response I'd like from you is 'Dear Honey Bear, I value and respect your right to regular high-performance styling treatments. I have made an appointment with my Hair Designer to discuss my follicular needs. I affirm and return your love and I validate your need for a shining 'do. Love, Poopsie.'

This is John Gray's response to the irascible tensions between the sexes. Havin' a big old whinge on bits of poorly decorated stationery. I'm rather enjoying tackling his Stencil For Self-Improvement, as it happens. I think I'll give it another go.

Dear Baby Harp Seal,

1. I am angry that you tipped bong-water all over my new napery.
2. I am sad that you haven't left me any mull.

3. I am afraid that you are so blunted when you visit Doctor Darryl that you often return home with half an ounce of dried coriander.
4. I am sorry about that time when you really wanted to go and see Frenzal Rhomb and I accidentally lost the car keys in the cat's sand toilet.
5. I love you and affirm your project of building a wading pool made entirely out of Gladwrap in the backyard.

Love, Pookie.

Yes, my name is Helen The Therapeutic and I'm patently working in the wrong industry! How helpful am I! Let's par-tay! Feed the world and let them know it's Christmas time! (Didn't anyone tell Bob Geldof that most of the people he was trying to save were actually of the Islamic faith where JC is only a piece of gum on Mohammed's more prophetic sandal? Or of some other creed where the Lord is really not an altogether important guy? Maybe they didn't give a shit that it was Christmas in Africa. Sheesh, the pure condescension of such missionary position charity gets up me. Why do these poor people always cop a lecture with their aid-subsidised millet? Why do we feel compelled to build a water pump AND bang on about how peachy keen our belief systems are?) Anyway, there's more people to help ...

Dear Angel Cakes,
1. I am angry that you have a porcelain figurines collection.
2. I am sad you have this bizarre predilection for shitty dolls in national dress.
3. I am afraid that you are in profound debt to the Franklin Mint people.

4. I am sorry that I undressed Miss Wales and Mister Sierra Leone and rearranged them in a lewd position.

5. I love you and I affirm your right to have really crap taste in things. But have you ever thought, perhaps, about philately or even commemorative teaspoons or just something a bit less embarrassing? I mean, my friends won't even visit us any more because every available flat surface is occupied by a fucking disgusting china Staffordshire bull terrier in a red tam o' fucking shanter. I mean, what is your case, you bitch? I can't break wind in my own home for fear of disturbing your repugnant vegetable shaped salt and pepper shakers and when we have sex these days, it feels like Kofi Anan Boutrous Boutrous-Ghali and the whole frigging UN contingent is looking at us in their bloody kilts, lederhosen and bolero jackets. You're really broken, you know that? You're really fucking whacked. You've even started colonising the back porch with swans made out of tyres, novelty Australiana and stupid fucking ugly concrete pelicans. It's like a cancer that will one day eat our house, me and the entire fucking suburb. If we buy a puppy or have children, will that help? Or will you just go completely bent and have them bronzed on arrival and put them in your fucking tasteless teak veneer Dolls Of The World display case? Oh look! There's Fido, John and Sarah standing next to the plastic Royal Edinburgh Cavalry In Ceremonial Dress. Let's give them a polish! One day I'm going to get a gun.

Love, your Little Dessert Fork.

If I delivered the recommended Anger, Sadness, Fear, Regret, Love and Invitation To Respond missive to my beloved, he'd call me a freak and then dump me. Quite justifiably, too. I think I wouldn't want to share my life and intimate hairy portals with someone who had to write me notes about how it hurts them when I use their protein rinse sans permission, so why should he? You don't really begin to understand how implacably fucked this Mars and Venus book is until you actually read it. With his REVELATORY (as if) statement that Men And Women Communicate Differently, Johnnie Gray invokes a sexual grammatology. Women need to be spoken to in a manner that addresses their need to be cherished. Men need to be spoken to in a manner that addresses their need to be needed. What? I just need to be spoken to in a manner that addresses my faculty for thought. He loves his fictional sexual difference, this bloke. It is significant, I think, that as men and women are learning to recognise and enact their similarities, a whole body of paranoid literature has emerged to dispute this development.

Contemporary 'relationship' pop psychology has emerged in this decade as a ravaged scion of the virulently diseased New Age Tree Of Life. Just as no-one told the hippies that actual thinkers had successfully posited the notion of human agency, nobody bothered to inform Partnership Counsellors that there had, in fact, been a feminist revolution. This is due in part, I feel sure, to the established fact that no-one likes talking to a wet, avaricious space cadet. There are probably all sorts of other essential discoveries of which they can boast no abstract know-ledge. The earth is not flat. Babies come from ladies' tummies. Madonna and Sean got a divorce, that type of thing. Reading the difference between the sexes as finite, biologically predestined and fixed is kind of like reading James Joyce's *Ulysses* and producing the critique, 'Well, that was a jolly good ripping tale about an odd Irish fellow who liked a drink! And that Molly Bloom, phew! Did she know how to talk or what?' Roland Barthes would have been rendered physically ill. That is, of course, had he not already been feeling quite under the weather as he was unconditionally squashed by a Parisian laundry truck in an instant of pure existential cruelty. I may have mentioned that before. Sorry. Whatever the bizarre circumstances of the demise of certain Franco-Algerian or French philosophers (hey, did any one else hear that thing about some Parisian punter falling out of a tree, breaking his neck and dying as the result of too much nihilistic glee at Sartre's funeral?), and whatever the textual fronds of *Ulysses* may resonantly reveal (Has anyone actually read that book?), I just wish people would stop being such thick tools. There's no excuse for it.

You have probably heard about Virginia Woolf. She's the overrated idol depicted in ladylike sepia profile on many feminist bedroom walls. (Incidentally, are there any sisters' army foot-soldiers or compassionate boyfriends out there who recall, as I do, the 'Feminist Bedroom' lifestyle break-out in pre-eminent UK harpie mag *Spare Rib*? It was piss funny and generally found somewhere between features on women in Northern Ireland, women in literature, women in chains and women in army disposal dungarees. It documented, as its title suggests, the boudoirs of assorted latter-day Boadiceas and usually read along the lines of: Fiona Cheese-Wheel, Who Has Rejected Her Patronym Of Legge-Smythe, Is Particularly Proud Of Her First Edition Radclyffe Hall Which Is Displayed On Her Recycled Cedar Reproduction Spice Rack Flanked By Her Extensive Essential Oils Selection And A Statuette Of Sappho. She Shares Her Buckwheat-Husk Filled Futon With Crisis Worker Lover,

Eldritch Gnome, And Upon It Occasionally Enjoys Performing Nonpenetrative Acts Of Empowering Lavender Love.) Ms Woolf, who truly copped the rough end of the phallocratic stick in her life, devoted some of her literary passion to an examination of fin-de-siècle gender travesty. That is, she wrote a book about a woman who often chose to frock-up as a bloke. We do not wear clothes, she advised in the saucy *Orlando*, rather, we are worn by them. The same may be said of gender. It may be sufficient to state, for the sake of certain individualist arguments, that we subjects simply slip comfortably into a prescribed gender identity as we ladies (or gents) would slip into a negligee. (Negligee, I think, is French for Next To Nothing. When we wear the negligee our gender becomes devastatingly and enticingly prevalent, and I don't just mean the rubber parts. Our overt gender is wearing us. We are being worn by next to nothing. Never are we so intimate with nothingness as when our gender is thoroughly enacted. Is Helen On Drugs, you may forthrightly ask. WHAT THE HELL AM I TALKING ABOUT?) While some believe we wear our gender, many other contemporary thinkers would believe the opposite. Gender robes itself in us. We do not figure centrally in the acquisition of our gender. The shape and the very substance of our selfhood are determined by the 'body' (or morphology) of our gender just as our entry to certain nightclubs is determined by the quality of our clothes. Well, now I'm just being silly! We do, however, drape our identity around the core concept of our gender. The construction of Man and Woman does not merely function, as the more enlightened hippies would have it, to obfuscate our 'true identity as people'. This understanding, dear, bored reader, is humanist pish! Our 'true identity' is manufactured and afforded by the very existence of gender. Identity demands this foundation of difference. Gender is like the floorboards and we are the matte finish. HAVE I MADE MYSELF CLEAR? (Oh, just shut up, Helen, and start talking about the telly or something actually of marginal interest.) Finally, without gender, 'we' cease to 'be'. Which probably explains why the author of *Men Are From Mars, Women Are from Venus* is so keen about detailing the 'fact' of biological differences between men and women. If he ceased to exist, he wouldn't be able to pick up his massive royalty cheques.

If my relentlessly undergrad meandering hasn't bored you into incontinence, you may actually be agreeing with me at this juncture. If this has occurred, you will presently be nodding and intoning 'Gender is bullshit, therefore identity is bullshit, so is my imputed existence, traditionally discerned as wickedly real, just more flagrant bullshit?' At which point, you will either (1) get impassive and, quite legitimately, turn to better and more challenging reading matter or (2) become irritated and actively seek a replacement for Descartes's cogito. I Blank (insert verb here), Therefore I Am. Personally, my sluggish cognitive powers have produced no splendidly docile nor expedient solutions. I Am Not. And, quite possibly, neither are you. I really hate life sometimes. It's just an uphill epistemological battle and lots of bad television. There are far too few answers and far too many channels playing infommercials for 'The Infinite Dress'. This amazing and, no doubt, highly flammable raiment wrought from some textile with a classification like Cellulose Crimplene Dacron (as used in the incendiary space shuttle *Columbia*) can be worn in over thirty different ways! (And they all look like shit!) If only existence was as darn drip-dry, resilient and versatile as this convenient wearable. What to do? Buy the infinite rig or just sit back and await the inevitable demise of gender, being and protracted cathode essays on the marvel of Tori Spelling's Fully

Automated Digital Ab-Cruncher In Three Designer Colours??
Within every foreboding grey cloud there lies …

Well, don't look at me like that. I scraped miraculously to a grim pass in Contemporary French and I completely fucked my Hegel exam. I know virtually nothing. All that I am certain of is that somebody invented some strange sexist shit a long time ago and it makes me and lots of other folks uncomfortable. Frankly, I am way too busy wondering why most boys I know have a higher credit card limit than me to truly address the prickly problematic of being. Furthermore, Australians are poorly equipped to properly wrangle with doubt. When you live on a Lenten, erstwhile gulag you tend toward certainty. The continued marginalisation and suffering of indigenous Australians, the withering away of equitable industrial relations and the presence of *Hey! Hey! It's Saturday* are conditions that tempt me to believe that somewhere, somehow, an ideologically circumspect superhero with good taste will arise to conquer my fears and save my shambolic country. Hardship turns you into an ideologue. The French are so much better at being errant nonbelievers. (Which probably explains why they invented nouvelle cuisine.) I think when you've got Provence, nice little cafes and a tractable, enviable health care system, doubt can be effected with the greatest possible poise. We've got the One Nation party while they can merely boast the occasional renegade laundry truck driver. I know who I'd rather get bludgeoned to death by. Mow me down, lorry boy.

None of this helps really, does it? I'm still an unreconstructed fool outlandishly obsessed with her credit rating and the varnish on her nails, so you can't expect much that is useful from me. I am decidedly not yet prepared to dispose of the 'evidence' of my own existence, so I can hardly expect anyone else to become a reeling, anarchic composition then, can I? I do sternly advocate, nonetheless, mentally preparing for the eventual decomposition of selfhood and our altogether unimaginable re-animation in a metagender landscape. The revolution, I have been advised, will arrive in due course. Fraught as this gargantuan shift will be, I suppose I'm looking forward to it. Any Old How, it's going to happen and no amount of frantic analysis, self-help or Infinite Dress purchase will stop it. For the moment, however, it is sufficient for us to enact minor notional movements in order to soften the eventual shock of waking one momentous day to find ourselves forlornly fleeceless and scattered randomly amongst the bedclothes.

Yes! You can begin exercising your postrevolutionary musculature today! By daubing a little systemic poison on the recently opened wounds of gender contusion you can immunise yourself against potential future rot. (In the postdeconstruction climate, symbolic order will be all distressed and botched up anyway, so mixed metaphors of the type just expressed will become more acceptable, meaningful and commonplace. It's not that I'm crap at writing or anything. Honestly!) If we concede (even momentarily, oh please) that gender provides a first principle and foundation for just about everything, we may be sure that it will emerge, come the crazy revolution, as the principal target for attack by the crazed, postmodern militia. As it's going to bugger off anyway, we should now begin to have a little constructive and fiendish fun with it. We can safely puncture, stretch and contort our masculine and feminine 'natures' without fear of meaningful reprisal. (This is similar to the gratuitous international direct dialling you perform when you know you're going to move out of your flat without first informing Telstra. Or drawing rude pictures of penises on a wall that you're shortly planning to paint. Or telling your boss to get fucked just before handing him/her that acrid letter of resignation stowed in your pocket.) The condition of being Man or Woman need not imprison us fully in the present. With a spot of intra-gender jolly high-jinks, we can subvent oppression, vigorously prepare the earth's paradigmatic intellectual surfaces for substantial change and, possibly, win those stupid breakfast radio competitions that purport to demonstrate the insoluble character of the 'Battle Of The Sexes'. History has afforded us a small, rare window of naughty pleasure. It would be remiss of us to neglect our obligation as the harassers of the past, the hedonists of the present and the helpful bestowers of tomorrow. SO, LET'S CROSSDRESS. I feel a fully patented, indispensable and world famous Never Fail Five Point Plan coming on.

HELEN'S NEVER FAIL FIVE POINT PLAN
FOR GENTLEMEN WHO WISH TO ENACT EXTREME GENDER TRAVESTY

1

Cry. Not only will this get you laid (one of my male colleagues elected to try weeping copiously in front of chicks when the news is on and he's been on an uninterrupted twelve month rod fest) but it will keep hippies off your back. Bearded blokes in socks and sandals won't invite you to their Let's Sniff Each Other's Bums, Smoke Cigars, Beat Drums And Howl About Our Fathers weekend forest retreats, cos obviously you're already sensitive enough. (And remember, when you start to feel like a wussy-boy, the Never Fail Five Point Plan has not been devised to get you 'in touch with your feminine side'. You may remain resolutely lager-bound and bladelike in many other realms. My scheme is only intended to help you mess with people's tiny heads. You must become powerfully epicene! Aim for the behavioural equivalent of a potent drag queen's ensemble. Not a wilted, Priscillaesque parody of femininity, but the genuinely confronting habits of one such as my comrade Vanessa Wagner. Vanessa always displays a tuft or two of virile chest whisker from beneath his/her florid viscose halter top.) Oh, if you're having trouble bawling, try a proven Pavlovian technique. Buy a relatively unobtrusive bell. Periodically ring it while subjecting your nasal hair to exorbitant yanks. Eventually, tears can be summoned via ding-a-ling. NB: It may prove a Herculean labour to do this undetected in the company of a Top Bit Of Sauce with whom you are reclining cosily opposite a video reproduction of *Terms Of Endearment*. I recommend borrowing *The Piano* from the video library, as it's a sooky movie in which the female lead does a shit-load of bell ringing. Befriend a merciful and compassionate film buff who can lead you to other Chick Flicks that include such frequent pealing.

2

Experience premenstrual tension. Obviously, this is going to be tricky. This may initially appear painful nonsense but, you know, just think of it as an adventure in virtual reality. To build a PMT simulacrum is possible. Eat a shrubbery's worth of cabbage and drink lots of extra gassy soda water so your gut blows up like the breast of a conceited bullfrog. Eat lots of sugary colon-hugging snacks several days in advance of the proposed simulation to (a) amplify abdominal discomfort and (b) outturn maximum spots-full-of-pus-on-the-face yield. On the evening before your ersatz ordeal, drink yourself into oblivion by means of Brandavino and Stone's Green Ginger Wine. The selfish distemper of the cheap hangover conjoined with spot-dehydration and fluid retention should heighten your charlatan condition. If you can somehow affix a burdensome weight to your lower stomach and manage a bit of back pain, you now have perfectly counterfeit bodily symptoms. Once you have completed your physical anamorphosis, it is time to reconstruct the powerful and involute emotions of the premenstrually tense woman. Begin, perhaps, by attempting to cram the memory of every person who has ever done you wrong into a five-minute interlude. Brood. Compare yourself to pictures of the doctrinally dishy. Gazing at Brad, Keanu, Skeet, Leonardo et al, moan, 'Oh I will never be so buff, rugged and peachy. I'm the ugliest boy who ever walked God's earth! Will anybody ever truly love a pig dog like me?' Tug your nose hairs and cry if you haven't already got the hang of the previously chronicled stimulus-response deal. Forge garbled relationship problems where there were none. Tell people unambiguously that you despise their every act and then arrogantly expect them to resile from your attack. When your victims refrain from humouring you and match your sour critique, shout, 'Nothing I do is ever fucking good enough!' Flounce. Resign from your occupation or course of study at least once over the five day period. You now have PMT. Congratulations. Reward your verisimilitude with further high-fat snacks. (The only obstacles to utter authenticity as far as I can judge are the gentleman's volition and his necessarily avowed culpability. That is, (1) women don't really 'choose' to be premenstrual and (2) women are generally unaware that their behaviour is in any way deviant. Diagnosis by women of their own PMT always comes as a big surprise! Despite a fairly textbook cycle in which I—her hum—egest modestly for five days and suffer preliminary complications for up to and including a further twenty, I consistently manage to forget that my rotten behaviour has got anything to do with my womb. Despite ingesting an unreasonable volume of cookie-dough ice confection, accusing my colleagues of mutiny and staring fruitlessly and disparagingly at my reflection, I am protected in my pellicle of denial. In the fifteen minutes of sanity that my twenty-eight day ordeal affords, I may recall the aplomb with which I tiger-punched my boss, tormented my house plants or macheted a bus stop. I then smile knowingly and say, 'Oh, I must have been pre-menstrual!') Proudly put out the flags of imminent ooze, dear gent reader, and enact the wild semaphore that will herald in a genuine, just and equitable sexual revolution.

3

Depilate. Fret about superfluous hair. Yes, I am aware that the majority of gents must scrape their strapping visages daily. I am also cognisant of the terror that unsightly upper-back tomentum may inspire in the adult male. And I urge you to understand that nobody was more aghast than me upon discovery of the horribly hispid and masculine-specific 'welcome mat'. (For the uninitiated, the term refers to the frequently profuse patch of hide located immediately upon the region of the lumbar vertebra. Nothing screams 'Down There Is My Freckle, Just In Case You Were Going To Miss It' with such ungainly and setaceous vehemence. Poor blokes.) As sympathetic to and intimate as I am with the unruly and often careening character of the male fleece, I urge aspirant gent-revolutionaries to immerse themselves in the feminine experience. Women are really weird about their fuzz. I, of course, prove no exception. Ladies, myself included, regard limbs that may be barely villiform with horror and immediately offer some sadistic fraulein fifty bucks to pour hot wax onto their pubescent down and then further distress terrified follicles by ripping them slowly apart. Ouch. Here again, our primary goal in realising gender transgression is not sought in the spirit of facile hippie artlessness. I do not wish for you, dear masculine reader, to Understand My Pain to any significant degree (although there is a minute, rarely charted enclave of my own luxuriant emotional hinterland that darkly aches to revenge several thousand years of stultifying Judeo-Christian patriarchal oppression, thanks very much. Perhaps let us resolve not to go there. Not without machinery, anyway). It simply would be, I venture, a fascinating exercise in effective mind-fuck technique for a modern lad to publicly evince an obsession for physical uniformity as pathological and wildly expensive as that of his female counterparts. I recommend a short-lived interlude of pilosity fixation in the male. Perhaps the procedure known in the aesthetician's coy lexicon as a 'French Wax' would be a circumspect beginning. This is the act of pruning the pubic mat into the shape of a valentine. Needless to impart, the French Wax can prove to be an exceedingly high maintenance downstairs styling choice. Your decision to emulate the feminine act of concentrating one's attention upon something that is rarely seen or appreciated will reverberate around the confines of our stinking world. Such harmless egotism can effect change! Further, the revelation of such a thing is stupendously comic and will easily win you bets down the pub.

4

Meddle. While male tribesmen authoritatively and unambiguously prescribe courses of decorous action, women are more covertly occupied as social and familial theorists. IT MUST BE CLEARLY STATED that, frankly, I detest the fey and fulsomely condescending conviction held by cranky mouldies that women, in fact, secretly and conspiratorially govern the universe. That Iron Fist In A Velvet Glove, Behind Every Great Man, Lead Us Into Servitude With A Glimpse Of Cleavage type of misogynist suspicion really shits me. The last time I bothered to look, the finance minister was a man. If he was 'unduly subjected' to strong but taciturn flirtatious feminine influence, maybe there wouldn't have been such a substantial swathe of cash excised from government subsidised childcare in the budget. However, I digress. (How darn unusual.) It is true that certain fulminating antiques are merely seeking impunity when they bang on about how women are the real powerbrokers (NB: These are the same bats who can be heard blaming the alleged lethargy of young 'uns for unemployment and Trotskyites for the diminishing quality of porridge oats.) These irksome dotards pursue the crudest possible technology to reason away the fact of their encroaching terror and doubt. Or perhaps there's just not enough roughage in some diets. I don't know. Having expressed all apologies, thereby outrunning the threat of an eternity spent in postfeminist perdition (which, I imagine, would be an unseemly torture. Camille Paglia on the fax machine all day, still bitterly transmitting to Julie Burchill. Endless melancholic tape loops of Tracy Chapman's Greatest Gender Non Specific Love Songs. Annie Sprinkle making everyone look at her cervix), I can get on with it. Women may have only minimal power. They do not possess control of much at all. They do try to meddle quite a lot, though. Despite the social coordinates that name me as Woman and therefore overwhelmingly unentitled to do anything socially, politically or economically significant with the exception of purchasing The Infinite Dress, I do tend to test the borders of my delimited influence. I try to fix things. It is of no consequence that I am lavishly misanthropic, indolent and horribly selfish. If I get wind of a fracture in somebody else's life, I'll sidle up and commence thrusting my inept paws into the bloody maw. Gentlemen should now begin to tinker with this, the sordid underbelly of absolute power. If a peer is tormented by a fissure in his or her primary personal relationship, give unsolicited and troublesome help.

Lecture vociferously about your world view, no matter how ill schematised, and the views of significant psychoanalytic thinkers, no matter how potty and inappropriate. As a meddlesome woman, I am presently attempting to dampen my effusive determination as a relationship hobbyist. I simply adore dispensing shitty advice. Blokes, by contrast, need to enhance their faculty for providing outlandish solutions to others' emotional conundrums. After a time you will find that it becomes impossible to staunch the relentless flow of obsolete refuse that gushes auto-altruistically from your mouth. (Those who have travelled extensively may have noted a similar propensity in natives of a particular province. There are folks who will loquaciously assist regardless of their qualification to do so ably. I have a profound fondness for perambulating about the Irish Republic, my ancestral home. However, I am always frustrated in attempts to navigate my way around its urban areas by means of verbal inquiry. Try asking a Dubliner in Grafton Street the way to Temple Bar. They will afford a charming social history of the area, indicate points of Georgian architectural interest and tell you how Bono has just bought another swanky nightclub there. They will refuse, however, to tell you what you need to know. But by that juncture you're probably so entranced by their lush verbiage you'll just want to pop off to their flat for an instant of Celtic, connubial, guilt-riddled bliss and attend a lecture with them afterwards at Trinity College entitled There Never Was A Potato Famine.) In any case, expansively proffer advice to everyone. Become the indispensable conduit for negotiations between disgruntled family members. At Christmas, Rosh Hashana, Ramadan or other potentially violent holy kin-fests, be that dependable stalwart with a supply of muscle relaxants, sedatives and touching, witty anecdotal diversions. If you deem it necessary, take a continuing education course in fundamental psychology and augment your personal development library so that you may dispense barely relevant admonishments and literature to those in obvious need. (NB: It is advisable to formulate a basic cataloguing system for books. Unsteady people are notorious for their inability to return things. I'm a big fan of reliable database software applications.)

5

Envelop. Now, of course there are entire suburbs full of women who stride about unimpeded by the need to smother. There are enviably autonomous jezebels who are more at home on a shooting range than within the swathed confines of a loving relationship. There are well-groomed gangs of towering neo-femmes who would rather forfeit their customer privilege as David Jones charge-card holders than spend two consecutive sentimental evenings in the company of a particular disposable mavourneen. However, to promulgate a process of freezing mutual absorption is traditionally understood as hard evidence of feminine specificity. It is now your goal, lucky gents, to thwart this belief by example. Commence by acquiring a small and faintly chucklesome ornamental dog. Liberally plash your new furry cosset with asphyxiating love. Animals such as the Cavalier King Charles Spaniel, the West-Highland Terrier or the chow-chow seem to effortlessly inspire stifling devotion in owners of either gender. It is far simpler to wetly favour a lap dog with endearment and treats than it is to benignly soothe an efficient working dog, such as the Australian kelpie. If you exchange your current economical, muscular, bone-masticating mutt for a sweet, sedentary spaniel who requires a pre-chewed dinner, humiliating admissions of toxic devotion will spew forth. Your introduction to a malumite-ine hair ball will transform you. Such a quadruped will take all the rank, cloying, anthropomorphising third-person tributes you feel capable to offer as in, 'Who's a good little furry boy? Frou-Frou the miniature French poodle is! Has he done his stinky? Show Daddy your fluffy flaxen bot bot! Non! Ne merde pas! He's a bad little Frou-Frou! Would he like a Belgian truffle and a Méthode-Champenoise enema, perhaps?' You just can't talk to a gleaming, sensible cattle dog in this fashion. They're far too bright and they spurn the adornment of pooch-parlour jingle bells and apricot ribbon. If you offered a blue heeler a diamante collar, a candy-pink chew toy or words of tender love, he or she would bite off large chunks of your leg. Find a dog that moves you to acts of unwieldy benevolence, care and grooming. Find a dog that you cannot, in all conscience, name 'Fang', 'Bluey' or 'Rover'. Once your coddled hound has thoroughly marshalled you, you are ready to subject yourself to abuse by actual humans. (As my homosensual gentlemen comrades are quite often already revolutionary either by default or by design, the following advice is geared primarily toward the hetero lad.) Use your most masochistic antennae to divine an insensitive, intolerant and troublesome mate. This may initially appear a tall order but you should take courage from the knowledge that scores of women have been expertly prospecting for and deftly mining these qualities in a mate for a good many years. All you really need is an abysmally fragile self-image and the ability to resourcefully browse your intended's index of inadequacy. Allusions to complete selfishness and an arduous demeanour are relatively simple to spy. If you have secured a pertinently disastrous partner, in the course of your first three avowedly romantic encounters you should be able to perceive a rapid decline in the volume and veracity of her sweet-talk. Such evanescence in a mate is pivotal for your purposes. By assignation number four, you should have visited the shops at her ravenous behest on at least three distinct occasions using only *your* monies. When a twenty-eight day era of vermeil, fraught togetherness has elapsed, you can be sure that you are on the road to obsequious victory if you are intimate with and have, indeed, voluntarily purchased both her preferred brand of feminine hygiene tourniquet and proven pharmaceutical or herbal prophylactic against uterine undulation. You may now have found yourself an appropriately impenetrable Cruella. If you are the sort who was formerly inclined to cathode entertainments such as the *I Posed For Playboy* telemovie or *Star Trek Deep Space 9*, congratulate yourself when you have become genuinely curious about the name of Jamie and Paul's new offspring in *Mad About You*. Ten further points are to be awarded if you can unhesitatingly recite the exact status of Julia's virginity, Charlie's syphilitic beard, Bailey's substance abuse problem and the street address of the Salingers' domicile in *Party Of Five*. Finally, if she tells you that your arse is too big for her tastes, leaves you panting on the brink of climax and then ebulliently sleeps with your sister before insensitively dumping you for a younger, thinner spunk, you have truly begun to emulate a sense of what it is to be female.

Cry with conviction and agility. Become bloated, irritated and premenstrually fraught on at least one occasion. Depilate with pathological abandon and keep an appealing geometric pubic fluff design in mind! Meddle with irrational intent. Envelop with reticular gusto. Well done. Reward yourself. You are now an emblematic transvestite. You are a crossdressing figurative beacon. Other blokes may be laughing but take courage! You are an androgynous connotative prodrome. You are a large, hairy hermaphroditic symbolic antecedent. You are an oracle of disorder. You are a parti-coloured harbinger of gender's demise. You are liberation made fascinating flesh. I want you! So do many others! I genuflect in your confusing presence. Viva la revolution.

HELEN'S NEVER FAIL FIVE POINT PLAN
FOR LADIES WHO WISH TO ENACT EXTREME GENDER TRAVESTY

1

Fiddle. Absent-mindedly 'rearrange' your primary sexual organ as often as possible. And do it in public for maximum deconstructive benefit. In *This Sex Which Is Not One*, eminent French feminist theoretician Luce Irigaray effusively traces the shape and 'morphology' of the twat in an effort to undermine the prevalent notion that woman's genitalia constitute a 'lack' rather than a presence. As swooning former attendees at seventies conscious-ness raising and vulval awareness morning teas may attest, the female sex organ can prove impossible to chart. As many lack-lustre paramours may further attest, the female sex organ can also prove impossible to navigate and adequately pleasure. We know little of the muffy's labyrinthinian character. The brush is not only macaronic but it is indomitable. The—her hum—nub of cata-clysmic quimdom may dodge its potential stimulus from encount-er to encounter. During one sweaty assignation, a woman may be content to simply have her clitoris affricated vigorously. During another, frissons of delight may be produced via the simultaneous means of (a) light, syncopated stroking of inner thigh with rare tern feather (b) judicious alternate relatively firm squeezing of left buttock and right earlobe with gloved hands and (c) *The Very Best Of Barbra Streisand* on the stereo. A woman's desire is perplexing, disordered and elusive. Her vagina is mazelike. Not only is the unassuming fur-burger knotted in a purely physical sense. Its function within the symbolic order is hard to pinpoint.

We all know how to spot a phallus. The Freudian term 'phallic symbol' now resonates in common parlance. A car or a handgun or a handsome, bevelled antique barometer may all be called 'phallic symbols' during heated domestic exchange as in 'stop dusting your phallic symbol and help me put out the garbage'. Such an accusation is deemed and, indeed, intended to be asperse. A woman wishes to indicate in conveying such a criticism that the man is driven by his ambition to demonstrate his own morphological proximity to the object he fondles, displays and adores. She is telling him, 'If you'll just stop fretting about male defined symbolic order for three seconds and help me with the fucking housework, your donger will not shrivel up and turn into a farcical flap!' And, of course, she would be right. I believe it was Jacques Lacan (a neo-Freudian at the Sorbonne from whom young, recalcitrant proto-post-modernist feminist woman scholar Luce Irigaray ran screaming) who developed the concept of the Phallus functioning as threshold signifier. All other 'things' in symbolic order are defined in relation to the Phallus. Men bear a special relationship to the Phallus as distinct from the tool. Gentlemen's willies, of course, bear a striking resemblance to the Phallus. This is why they get paid more, have fewer headaches and are less indecisive when confronted by the potentially limitless possibilities of an open wardrobe. The vagina, by contrast, merely sits there sluggishly, darkly and conspicuously absent. There are no 'Vaginal Symbols' other than those lacunae and gaps that terrify us and that we choose not to adequately explain. The Infinite Dress is possibly a vaginal symbol. So are nervous breakdowns, hissy fits and parfait desserts. But I digress (again, knock me down with a rare tern feather). If women persist in scratching, unfolding and boasting about their 'gashes' (eurgh, a wound inflicted by the true piercing might of the threshold signifier), a new semiotics of feminine specificity may conceivably follow.

2

Nudify. Here again we have an opportunity to demystify the tangled vagina. Nuding up allows further exploration of and potent symbolism for the 'dark continent' of female desire and rubbery bits. In flagrantly positing the evidence of one's proscribed and delimiting gender classification, one begins to thwart the machinery of patriarchy. Also, nakedness is piss funny. Streaking publicly may possibly afford women a heretofore neglected dalliance with delight. Overly shod sisters, have you never envied the joy with which antipodean gents enact the moon, the browneye, the fruit bowl (back view of a browneye), the pressed ham (naked arse held against a transparent pane), the prancing pork rind (pressed ham in rapid vertical or horizontal motion), the braniac (scrotum bisected by means of undergarment) or flies eyes (same thing, really, but faintly more repugnant)?? I insist upon reclaiming my right to comical nudeness. Why is a female streaker discredited and sexualised at a large outdoor sporting event? It is not just that a jaunty jiggling nature girl should suffer the slings and arrows of rapacious punters while a lad is esteemed as a noble and amusing savage. It is my fear, however, that some unclad women wish only to be desired. Looking like a stacked, cherishable porn princess is not the issue here. The feminine nudist must not summon images of Tracii Lords, Helena Christensen and lean pure turkey meat before she displays herself in the altogether. Stark fatuous cheesecake is not your key to empowered dismantlement. Dishabille must be performed in a manner that is at once chucklesome and asexually, awesomely and unapologetically rude. Rather than informing your imminent naturist performance with thoughts of stick flicks, supermodels and lustrous, lickable flesh, it is far wiser to examine the dishelming habits of the man who performed what was arguably this country's greatest ever pants-drop, Barry Crocker. In the stagnant, wilfully sexist, wholly chauvinist motion picture *The Adventures Of Barry Mackenzie*, Baz treats the world to a peek at his date. And, lo, what a funny quoit it is. (The film's protagonist is rewarded bonus points as this memorable arse disfurnishing was performed in front of British people.) Mr Crocker defiantly stands regally upon a makeshift podium, turns backward and flashes his freckle while arhythmically waggling. It is a moment of unmitigated comic perfection. It is also profoundly poignant. Baz has just been asked to provide marginal gloss on the proclivities of his country men and women. Unable to communicate the Australian national character eloquently by orthodox verbal means, he elects to instead display his twin furry lobes. The word has become articulate flesh. This constitutes a watershed moment in Australian cultural history and should be assiduously studied by young women who wish to replicate its significance. Another divesting notable from which you may derive lewd instruction is wily five-eighth Laurie Daly. There is hard documentary evidence of Laurie's post 89 Grand Final fan dance. If you have the contacts to procure a videotape of this pediment performance by the most exquisite cog in the Green Machine, I suggest you exploit them fully. Rugby league fans and winsome women everywhere marvel as the pre-eminent Canberra 'Milk' Raider drops his daks after first imparting 'I told yez all that I'd flog meself if we won the Cup! So I will!' He then proceeds to drop his capacious club shorts, grab his barely tumescing member in his right hand and demonstrate its use as an exceedingly comic prop. There's a spot of salacious nut work that goes on also, but I will spare you from my slavering rendering. Finally, in a pure instant of perspicuous nude-expressionist camaraderie, a Canberra front-rower assists Laurie in his tugging verisimilitude by standing at his side and wantonly spraying the congregation with frothy, excitable beer. It is rumoured that our former prime minister Bob Hawke was among the aspersed assembly. Pure magic. I long for a time when all things, and most especially going buff, form just one mammoth pile of undifferentiated ooze. I dream of a day in which my vagina is authentically mirthful. Why does woman feel compelled to make her exposure lascivious? Why has she not yet attained the confident technology of gigglesome self-defoliation? Why are men the only folk presently evincing daring pressed hams in speeding vehicles? We must vow, sisters and comrades, to responsibly nude-on.

3

Let fluffy off the chain. Men are rarely prudish where matters of bodily emissions are concerned. I find the punitive feminine attitude toward belching, rectal gas leakage, ear wax, pus, snot and odd sebaceous oil difficult to understand. Ladies, as mentioned previously, are not in morphological possession of an organ that bears proximity to symbolic order's threshold signifier. Without a meaningful phallic frond, women are thereby excluded from a similarly meaningful inclusion in symbolic order. Feminine beings are, accordingly, construed as merely physical, while men waft about nonchalantly in a metaphysical realm. Women can only participate in literal acts of expression. Men are capable, by contrast, of being figurative. Given this bizarre, dichotomous arrangement where women are identified with the body and men are exemplary of the mind, it's odd that women don't admit to farting more often. Don't you think? Perhaps it is because of, rather than in spite of, men's attested cognitive trajectory from their 'nature' that they are happy to grin after breaking wind and proclaim, 'It was me, huh huh!' Men confidently assume that they have effected the Cartesian mind-body split. And so they are able to view their flatulence objectively. Blowing off stands merely as a tragicomic reminder of how far they have been transported from their 'primitive origins'. Women, by contrast, live in constant entrapment to their alleged natures. As the male is comfortably and positively defined as the enviable masculine phallus-bearing metaphysical One, the female attempts to outrun her status barely and negatively defined as an old neglected trolley full with pathetic feminine phallus-lacking physical Otherness. The oppression and discomfort that such a definition implies for women motivates their attempts to thwart it. To illustrate, when a woman expels methane flotsam, she runs the simultaneous risk of discharging the evidence of her enslavement to the body. If a gent shoots a similar fairy, it is merely an amusing testimony to his complete mastery of the body. It takes a fearless vixen with a developed sense of impunity to perform the Blue Flame (or, indeed, the quaint interpretive Dance Of The Flaming Arseholes) in polite company. Women are reluctant to account for or detail the progress of their various bodily suppurations, eructations, pellets, evictions and hurls. In times past, the few women that have been considered remarkable by the dominant, masculine standard were commonly troubled fruit-bats who managed some alleged transportation from their bodily mess. The Virgin Mary, of course, is famous for allowing only an amorphous God to fiddle with her downstairs accoutrements. She is loved for being an impenetrable and immaculate porcelain vessel who ovulates only when the Lord gives the holy go-ahead. Joan of Arc is noted for her bizarre vision quest. She could 'see' beyond our mere physical realm. She was relatively untroubled when the pile of brittle kindling at her feet was torched. What a loop. (In my unscholarly reading of Joan-dedicated texts, I have come to the conclusion that this churlish European teenager was more than likely a chronic anorexic whose hallucinations were prompted by a lack of substantial nourishment. Contemporary eating disorders in women may therefore be similarly viewed. Active self-imposed starvation multiplied by exceeding bodily disdain cubed equals notoriety plus an outlandishly enhanced and distended sense of power and possibly a nice suit of armour. It makes some irksome kind of sense to view the late twentieth century practice of sticking the fingers down one's ladylike throat as a response to the threat of feminism. When confronted by the possibility of monu-mental change, there are always those who would rather die in their attempts to exceed it.) Men will graphically and boastfully recount their excursions in technicolour yawning while women will contrive some barely feasible synthesis of the truth to explain their forty-five minute absence. Further, men will self-aggrandise by loudly chronicling details of their merest concupiscent 'con-quest'. A proper lady would not think to offer the details of her ordeal. Squirt for squirt, it must be said, during the course of an average lifetime women may decidedly lay claim to having more numerous and interesting bodily secretions than men. Terrified that they will sink into the primordial prelinguistic oozing and purely physical morass that is the currently dominant masculinist understanding of femininity, women devote a lifetime to perform-ing, staunching, excusing and neglecting their manifold dis-charges. We must refuse the antiquated dichotomous belief system that causes us to blame others for our wind. We will be con-ceptually severed from our joyously belching brothers no longer! By refusing to aimlessly tread the treacherous molasses that contains our prescribed, polite and proper feminine identities we prepare for the next thoroughly golden millennium. Women must become as able as men to evoke hilarious genito-urinary jests and cathartic scatological japes. Do not be subsumed by the myth that your body defines you. Treat it with tender disrespect and good humour. (A gentleman acquaintance of mine employs a radical flatulence methodology that may prove of interest to the eager femme. On long elevator rides—Centrepoint Tower for example—some passenger is bound to egest wind due to the unfamiliar sensations of vertical speed and excitement. When no brave soul claims responsibility for the pungent dispersal, bravely confront your captors and proclaim unabashedly, 'It was mine!' Appropriating boastful authorship of another's noisome shame can prove both excessively amusing and deliciously liberating. There is also the enduring classic of 'Pull My Finger' to fiendishly attempt. Further, swimming pools, jacuzzis and bathtubs or other finite bodies of shared water are sodden with lewd comic potential. You are now bereft of excuses. Stride forth and make your unctuous, piquant mark, ladies.)

4

Drink beer. I am chummily aware that many of you already do so competently and voluminously. Sadly and inexplicably, however, certain faulty niche-marketing wizards appear to have overlooked this happy fact. Advertising campaigns persist in directly addressing a primarily female market when purveying their execrable alcoholic lolly waters (merely tarted up wine coolers, as mentioned previously in the Crankiness Template). Further, and I personally find this a more incisive affront, inferior beers with a rough, overweening bead, a distinctly Issey Miyake-esque bouquet and a saccharine sensation that is long on the palate are occasionally peddled to us chicks. (Some of you may recall that a specific tawdry lager with the word 'Sydney' in its title tried to synthesise a female constituency and failed.) Why should we not be flagrantly proffered the opportunity of savouring a fine beaded, malty, impertinently bitter ale with a bouquet redolent of discarded blue work jerseys and discerning upper palate notes of the farmyard? Aaah, an age-old symphony that is gratifying and replete with a hint of mare's bottom. In my relatively short life I have enjoyed heavies, bitters, milds, porters, scrumpies, lagers and hops-heavy Czech pilseners. I made it a point to seek and consume the Teutonic brew weiss beer. (A mouth-watering ale concoction derived from the German wheat crop.) Many women are known to me who are quite so assiduous in their pursuit of an informed beer palate. Those assorted coy temptresses that declare, 'I can only have half a glass before I feel completely bloated!' are simply performing their conspiratorial duty as the crypto-servants of men. Fey and vexatious sweetie-pie nuisances, your expulsion from this earth is nigh. Sometimes I do wonder if upholding the phallic ideal is a mere habit. Would a vast fissure appear in the planet's crust to swallow us whole if we were to synchronously challenge by unambiguous example the alleged differences of man and woman? Would the finger of God poke us into crumbling irrelevance if we were to order a Guinness and, gasp, drink it alone at the bar? Would men really mind that much if we swaggeringly demanded, 'Oi, Tiger, get us a schooie while you're up.'? Probably one or two of the violently thick ones would. For the most part, however, I conjecture that a frosty would be delivered to your table without a glimmer of askance. (The only oblique suspicious look you may attract is in the case that you neglect the next shout. Or should you pollute your beer with a lesser effervescence to make it shandy. I repeat my admonishment. Do not prettily admit to feeling 'bloated' or you will be duly ejected from the public house. Does a gentleman complain of such a malady? No! Men are proud to be bloated. As it happens, many of them spend studious hours in the pub in pursuit of a bloated status.) Further, as earlier studies prove there are different inebriated therapeutic modalities. That is, lolly water and wine coolers turn you into a despicable fractious armadillo, bourbon and brown spirits in general make you bellicose (and, possibly, truculently morose and comatose), white spirits and vodka in particular can transform you into a shrieking automaton, red wine enhances the faculty for mawkish bombast, cocktails will whip you into an insubstantial froth, chardonnay produces a tortured boring ponce, verdelho dehydrates your charm to a raisin-like pellet, port causes you to vote Liberal and crave austere leather, sherry is a trifling fortification that excises your Nietzschean Will To Power, rosé ensures that your conversation will become overwhelmingly insipid, champagne alternately ripens the gonads into yearning fullness and mashes the head with a beaded mallet, schnapps gives birth to a haphazard Bolshevik, and Stone's Green Ginger Wine will ensure your eventual emergence as an indigent, chunder-streaked derro. Beer just causes you to sing rugby union ballads! Relatively harmless, if you think about it. Quite simply, beer is the only refreshment in which the responsible tippler should regularly indulge. So, you get a little bit expansive and crude! You may want to pull down your pants and incandescently blue-flame away. However, if you have carefully studied point three in the Never Fail Five Point Plan For Ladies, you will acknowledge that this only adds to the index of this beverage's many positive benefits. Moreover, men find themselves far better prepared to perform their own recommended steps toward gender travesty when they have a gutful of ale. You should become drinking buddies with beer drinking boys as you wouldn't want to miss their Guinness-driven attempts to copiously weep about their unresolved Oedipal conflict, now would you??

5

Gamble. Well, actually, I despise gambling. It's a virulent stinky ill. The two unshriven gaudy temples built in its honour are, of course, Star City and the Crown Casino. Star City is a blight on Sydney Harbour, distending its soft, lenient, gorgeous sandstone trim and defiling the memory of its original owners. Further, the edifice boasts a lurid, marine-motif carpet that must have been designed by an acid casualty interior architect. And spirits are six hefty bucks. As far as the Crown's aesthetics are concerned … well, nothing is going to render the Yarra less repugnant. One cannot, as the popular homily proceeds, polish a turd. Similarly, one cannot deface that which is already resolutely turdlike. Nonetheless, the Crown Casino stands as crass testimony to Jeff's populist, quick-fix, imbecilic economic problem solving. I cannot pinpoint the usefulness of either establishment. Okay, so they provide state revenue. When you posit this fiscal advantage against the torment of casino-generated unemployment and despair, however, the community and public sector's resources will be tried beyond present day financial feasibility. I personally have, I am told, a genetic predisposition to gambling. One of my great-grandfathers, it is reputed, walked into Port Phillip Bay and drowned himself rather than confront his creditors. (He left behind an ailing business, a frail wife and five destitute children. Two of the kids became certifiable later in life. Cowardly old sook.) This is the worst of it. There are less hefty, more lambent gambling narratives in my family history. My father, for example, has been deploying his digitally enhanced 'system' on the nags for nigh on thirty years. In 1968 he told my mother that he would take her on a revivifying second-honeymoon-type excursion to Hawaii on the proceeds. Tired of waiting, Mum bought a garden centre and took me to Ireland instead. Essentially, you can never win. However, certain forms of gambling are held in high masculinist esteem. So I suggest that ladies merely pretend to gamble. They should do so down at the track. Hippomania is considered to be equal parts valour and maths. Pokies or cardies are not enough. Such trifling forecast is the province of wimps to the gaming elite. Like Freud's infant analysand Little Hans, many blokes have a thing for horses. Women should reactivate their pre-pubescent pony fascination and acquire one too. I suggest that ladies deftly familiarise themselves with racing terminology post-haste. Quinella, Trifecta, Quadrella, Totalising, Favourite and the Marking Of One's Book. My father, who remains an Oahu hopeful, informs me that other useful phrases are pacemaker, miler, sprinter, stayer, the persuader, swishing the tail, railing, gone via the cape, each-way, swoop, racing plates and, finally, my two preferred and overused terms, Send Out A Lantern (or 'Where the fuck is my horse?') and Next Comes Daylight (or 'Finally, there's my fucking horse!').

Ladies, you must learn to fiddle. Do not fiddle with the frustrated, poignant desire of a convent girl who knows what she's doing is wrong in the eyes of the Lord. As much exhibitionist pleasure as it may afford to masturbate in the presence of an impotent deity, stop it at once. Be more nonchalant! Fiddle with the pusillanimous abandon of an Australian spin bowler. Remember that an ill-gotten climax is not always your objective. Perform irresolute origami with your netherfolds. Disrobe not with the distressed urgency of a motley Kings Cross fan dancer but with the comic integrity of an ample, gangling male sports-ground streaker. Fart not with the repressed denial and pain of a Tory politician who is paddled by a buxom madam in cloying weekly privacy. Fart with the loud avuncular dignity of an adipose publican. Drink beer not with the tentative chagrin of a shandy-sipping befrocked matron. Imbibe it instead with the gusto of a fighter pilot returned to Queensland from a trying tour. Finally, gamble on the gee-gees. Or at least pretend to. This will be very sassy, indeed. The revolutions will be galvanised.

CHAPTER EIGHT

LEARNING TO ACHIEVE BETTER HEALTH BY EFFECTIVELY HATING AND DECONSTRUCTING THE MEDIA (WITH PARTICULAR REFERENCE TO 'HEY! HEY! IT'S SATURDAY')

Now, you may wish to turn to Noam Chomsky, de Saussure or Jacques Lacan for a more thorough explication of mass-produced signs. If that is the case, get thee to a quality bookshop at once and spurn lewd, fractious paperback-only publications with unapologetically publicity-seeking expletives in their title such as the one you now cradle in your work callused hands. You deserve so much better. My only qualification for addressing this topic (apart from my incomplete, ultimately disastrous, semiotics top-heavy degree) is my occupation as a mass electronic media commentator for some eight fraught years. Of course, my entire term has been spent in the employ of the Australian Broadcasting Corporation. An edifice better known, perhaps, for its fortuitous staff meal allowance initiatives and an inexplicable allegiance to irksome, caterwauling modern opera than for its Murdoch-style union-bullying and incisive media savvy. However, if my pot-holed faculty for recent memory is any index, I can't recall the last time Red Symons' published a treatise entitled 'Pluck-A-Duck And Feathery Hermeneutic Play: Does This Anthropomorphised

Bird Challenge Predominant Assumptions Held By Mainstream Australia Regarding Poultry Or Is He Just A Bloke In A Non-specific Duck-Suit?' in an Australian academic quarterly. But then again, I've been so busy setting a new world record for playing Riven without a fucking clue (and trying to find my way out of the great revolving room and onto the crest of the golden dome where, I am told, there will be a coloured stones puzzle that, if I can summon my lateral powers and untangle it, just might stop the steam from clouding the peephole on that weird bronze cone-oid thing next to where that bloke who looked like a Shinto priest got iced in the first five seconds) that there's a lot of stuff I miss. (Why I torture myself so, I have no idea. I estimate that this very title would have been completed some two years earlier had it not been for that cruel piece of binary hippie shit known as Myst. I was pleased to hear that Trent Reznor similarly blames the advent of Doom for his continued Nine Inch Nail-ed non-presence on the Dark Industrial front.) Whatever the case, in the absence of a substantial participant-observer body of text that directly addresses the pish that is popular Australian media, I guess you'll just have to deal with me.

It may come as no significant shock to learn that most people who work in the media are stupid fucks. Just how thuddingly thick may remain a mystery to many of you. Some years ago one of my colleagues was tickled to encounter a senior staff member with a regional broadsheet whose cruel parents had christened him James Joyce. This colleague of mine—a jolly and pleasingly rubicund fellow who had, no doubt, paused only to make jokes about Stephen Dedalus and how terrible it must be to have a loony wife and was the rumour about him writing *Finnegan's Wake* entirely on library slips true?—immediately called his own news editor to share the joke. 'Who's James Joyce?

A union front-rower? I'm from Melbourne. I only follow the AFL,' came the reply. One may forgive a pharmacist, a fruiterer or a forensic scientist this sin of literary omission. Some people simply don't need to know who the hell James Joyce was. (As I have posited in other texts, if Sylvia Plath had never encountered Joyce's work at university, perhaps she wouldn't have married that pathetic loser Ted Hughes and gone on to stick her head in the oven.) News editors, however, NEED TO KNOW. This poor sod editor. Once word travelled of his mammoth and debilitating ignorance, many of us would ask questions like, 'When they say Gulf War, do they mean the Gulf of Carpentaria, or is it somewhere in Latin America?' Or 'Who is Bosnia Herzegovina?' or, more pointedly, 'Hey Dickhead! How many fingers am I holding up?' Following some spectacular professional hiccup of Dan Quayle-esque proportions involving East Timor and some copy that was broadcast referring to the 'Dilly Bag Massacre' he slouched off. I think he went on to become a ministerial press secretary for the federal Liberal party. I heard it was something to do with a defence policy portfolio. I alacritously engaged the services of an esteemed industrial architect to design me an invasion-proof nuclear fallout shelter for the back porch. Sometimes I can't sleep for the fear.

I could recount many other travesties. Sadly, the threat of litigation prevents me from doing so freely. Suffice it to say that I have watched the most intellectually unencumbered dunderheads imaginable scale the towering, mirrored, slippery cenotaph of corporate excess. I have observed aghast and in painful silence the extermination of genuinely functional minds. Pure intelligence is as effusively and thoroughly pursued and punished as 'communists' were by the random, paranoid and ultimately self-serving McCarthy-led House Un-American Activities crap shoot.

In the electronic media maelstrom, women are inexplicably prized for their modesty, their modulation (Who wants to hear a shrill harpie, Helen?) and their ability to construct a comfy, nurturing nest to coax spectacular flight from their downy, precocial little boy baby birds. People of colour are valued for their ability to testify the fact of a cynically polyethnic managerial policy. Gay men and lesbian women are employed for their 'perverse' comic appeal. And the differently abled? Well, apart from an apologetic coverage of the Paralympics, just fucking forget it. The only minority that actually directly benefits from the stinking, wretched electronic media refuse heap is that consisting of the consummately stupid. You've got to be thick to happily consume media and thicker still to succeed within its confines.

Many believe that the acquisition of adulthood is characterised by a process of disenchantment. If this is the case, then I am very mature indeed. I am moribund with the ceaseless mitigation of my youthful and artless naivete. As a child I always admired journalists and other media commentators as creatures of great rock-and-roll valour, cognitive prowess and integrity. Now I realise that the only portion of the hard-bitten news-hound stereotype they choose to actively embody is scandalous alcoholism and fetishistic, egoistic sex acts.

One need not be enslaved as an employee of the media to fully surmise its corrupt and ineffable silliness. One is simply required to hit the button marked 'on' located, generally, in the top right hand corner of one's remote ignition device and confront the cathode interface at six-thirty on a Saturday evening. The Channel Nine network, and affiliated aggregated stations, naturally:

HEY! HEY! IT'S BOLLOCKS

One is greeted by some unconvincing, promotional tour mimics who flail their paste-on dreadlocks to the muffled-for-family-viewing thudding of their latest chart-topping hit which is eerily transmitted at studio quality. Odd that they can play with such agility, seeing as how they usually seem so unswervingly blunted by executive record company provided narcotics. (Well, you'd want to punch out that dickhead with the saxophone too if someone hadn't got you truly fucked up first.) If the minstrels dare to step beyond the boundaries of that which has been Packer-ratified as Seemly Rock Behaviour, then the next thing you see is a bouf-fanted, ape-ish host who coldly instructs his seratonin-deficient studio audience NOT to applaud. 'Don't applaud. They are a very unprofessional group and they're obviously on drugs,' Daryl is famously alleged to have said after an appearance by ebullient, shaggy British blues rockers and general good-time boys, Reef. Well, of course they were on drugs, Dazza! How else would they have been convinced to appear on your noisome, irrelevant Variety Show? (May I impart that I have met with Reef and indeed enjoyed their live acoustic radio performance immensely. Never have I encountered such gorgeous devil-may-care sweetly sardonic and lavishly pants-dropping pop stars. Moreover, the lovely little boy vocalist actually refused my offer of lager in case it affected his performance. Needless to impart, they profitably employed their time on the radio to squeal 'Hey! Hey! It's Bollocks' with comic regularity.) Daryl has become notorious for his sidekick shuffling. When supremely effervescent Rhodes scholar Jacqui Macdonald left to pursue a career in servitude to her anomalously geometric hairstyle, veteran Melbourne comed-ienne Denise 'Ding Dong' Drysdale was subpoenaed as a witness to Daryl's attested media magic. Ding Dong's destiny as Daryl's sous-clown was short-lived. Possibly because she became justifiably righteous regarding all the jests aimed at her well-upholstered bosom. More than likely, she was too damn interesting. (Things in ponds, you know. I've seen lichen more erratically arresting than Daryl Somers.) With the advent of regular, satisfying sexual congress in my life, I lost a little interest in proactively loathing *Hey! Hey! It's Bollocks*. I am informed that, post-Ding Dong, a number of sterling co-hostesses auditioned for the honour of performing televised metaphoric fellatio upon Mr Somers. Ms Jo-Beth Taylor was successful. A clanswoman of mine informs me that, at the time of writing, Ms Taylor is seriously ill and that it may be in poor taste to critically chronicle her history as an entertainer. I will simply say that she began public life as a back-up singer for Indecent Obsession (putatively heterosexual, largely forgotten, late eighties blond pop atrocity from Brisbane, direct ascendants to Savage Garden, discovered by Molly Meldrum). She later went on to chortle her way through *Australia's Most Virulent, Obtuse, Violent And Professedly Funniest Home Videos*. Poor lamb. Another discarded filament of the *Hey! Hey!* fabric is, of course, Ossie the pink ostrich. In my gormless, halcyon university days, I must confess I was not above chuckling at the antics of this roseate toy feathered-fledgling. Ossie was all instinctual impulse and desire. He gave the program an id. This is evident by the choice of his breed. The ostrich is a churlish, stupid and cowardly bird notable for shoving its head into the sand at the first sign of danger. In a surprising act of metaphoric disassembly, Ossie's creators obviously had this in mind. Ossie was an emblem of the fear-dodging ostrich reborn, phoenixlike, from the ashes of comfort. When terror encroached, Ossie identified it, as in, 'Daryl, your hair just seems to get bigger!' He functioned in the *Hey! Hey!* text as a blush and blush-making avowal of fundamental human need. Rather as Satan does in the Old Testament, as physical love does in the work of William Blake, as the 'Noble Savage' does in Jean Jacques Rousseau's schematised anthropological account of human development, *The Origin Of Inequality,* and much in the way that Coco Pops do in the supermarket breakfast cereal aisle. I, as stated previously, have serious notional objections to the concept of a Jungian pre-existing 'id', or indeed to any other phrenic models that allege the anteriority and immutability of human desire. However, I miss Ossie Ostrich. What kind of fuckwit gives a fluffy damask bird puppet the arse? Daryl Somers, that's who. And who invented Red Faces? This portion of the show, sponsored by McDonald's Family Restaurant Franchise, produces some titian faces indeed. Nothing is more desirable to the *Hey! Hey!* production team than the humiliation of young, plump children. Amateur performances by 'real' members of the public, which may evince cosy charm at family barbecues, are detonated by Red Symons with his use of what poses as 'acerbic wit'. Patently, Symons still bears the scars inflicted by an ungainly, unprepossessing infancy. Obviously, our hard-won advertising dollar would be better expended on his thorough and uncompromising neo-Lacanian psychoanalytic rehabilitation than on his elevation to the status of August Cynic. He is not a cynic. Robert Hughes is a cynic. He writes notable books about his suspicion of postmodernity. Luce Irigaray is a cynic. She writes beautiful prose poems to imaginary philosopher lovers underscoring both the undocumented rites of feminine specificity and the myopia of phallocentricity. Phillip Adams is a cynic. Granted, it's about time he changed out of that black turtleneck he must have purchased from a 'funky' menswear store in the very early seventies, but at the very least he documents his prolonged critique of talk-radio annihilationists via means of text.

Red Symons should just shut the fuck up and stop making little kids unhappy. He should simply concentrate upon that at which he is adept. Playing mediocre session guitar in an uninspiring house ensemble and obscuring his embittered, florid face. As for Pluck-A. Well, he is no match for the incendiary sarcasm of the absent ostrich. He is no oracle who voluntarily plucks his head from the desert floor to astutely confront his oppressors. No! He's a man with his head resolutely shoved right up a duck's arse. Pluck-A is an idiomorphic mute puppet who proffers charitable gifts to the poor without addressing the origins of real need. He is the Bob Geldof of puppets. And I suppose, what with all her quaint and outlandish dirty talk, that would make Paula Yates the Ossie Ostrich of celebrity. There is also Molly. Are we supposed to believe that Madonna actually makes up the sofa bed for him? My Aunty Kath knows more about the vicissitudes of contemporary music than this old palaver-profferer, and the last record she bought was Val Doonican's *Christmas Songs Of Praise*. Week after week he returns to endure the poofter-bashing of the voice over boot-boy, whose snide 'insightful' axioms I do not have the strength here to discuss. (As for the sound effects genius who seems predestined to engage a toilet flush for every circumstance and the crude cartoonist who evidences all the careful humour of Kevin 'Bloody' Wilson with a packet of Derwents. Primordial grunts will only suffice to convey my consummate disdain.) When will this balding self-professed benefactor take off his frigging mouldy cowboy hat and retire? Why does he persist in baring his wan parchment arse to receive the supposedly affectionate swipes of orthodox disapproval? Why the artless record company idiots continue to fruitlessly furnish him with extreme, high-cost junkets is simply beyond my ken. NOBODY bought the last Prodigy record because Molly suddenly pronounced that techno was cool.

All that Ian achieves is to rob respectable recordings of their initial meaning and resonance. He coaxes, perhaps, a few misguided parents into purchasing hideous items for their aghast progeny. Nobody listens to Seattle any more, thanks, Dad, you wilful naif. Why, why, why Molly, you nauseating, doddery old Uncle Tom of (allegedly) gay men? Why Daryl? Why Red? Why Pluck-A? Just fucking stop it and put wildlife documentaries on Saturday evenings instead. I'd much rather watch a jaguar ravage an unsuspecting zebra than tolerate this contemptible theatre of the absurd and woefully idiotic.

I have here employed the use of *Hey! Hey! It's Saturday*'s flawed textuality to indicate all that is wrong with broadcast. And that which is wrong with Australian broadcast in particular. This feigned, imposturous entertainment manifests all that is rotten within the media and its concomitant culture. Disapproval, paternalism, Lenten despair, homophobia, impoverished humour, cruelty, deceit, flagrant racism and blokes who like shoving their heads up the dupable arses of inculpable waterfowl. It's all displayed there pulsing feebly in twenty-seven inches of lurid, putrescent colour. While our continued and formally stated objection to Hey! Hey! It's Bollocks is paramount, we cannot be blinded to lesser media misdemeanours. *Hey! Hey!* is, and shall likely remain, the quintessential noxious swill in whose consistency we may divine all manner of motivation to importunate epistolary. (NB: When complaining, as I recommend you do, do not reveal your hand right away. Do not begin the negative communique to Channel Nine's Chief Executive Officer with 'Dear Jamie Packer, Just because fucking Kate fucking Fischer fucking agreed to fucking marry you and you fucking may have shagged Jennifer fucking Flaivin and you've fucking got a fucking big chin and a fucking swish fucking Bondi fucking flat and your fucking dad put you in fucking total fucking charge of the fucking known fucking world.' Okay?) As I have advised in other media, always whinge wisely, vehemently and in a manner that demands both a serious appraisal and response. It is possible that you are overwhelmed by potential complaint and currently sedentary in your capacity as enraged consumer. It is with this in mind that I proffer a list of a further twenty media demons you may wish to annihilate.

1. *Sabrina The Teenage Witch*. Like *Bewitched* before it, *STTW* manages to excise all the untreated dirty sex and feminine specificity from witchcraft mythology. Like Ellen Degeneres's out lesbianism, Rachel's (from *Friends*) retail addiction and Rhoda's flamboyant dress sense, Sabrina's supernatural power merely functions as a comic obstruction. It is the device that is frequently called upon to underpin her soft fluffy gorgeous feminine humanity. Such a device represents sitcomic hyperrealist morality at its very worst. The flaw, sexual proclivity or chortlesome addiction is portrayed as something which must be overcome or obfuscated. This desire to manfully erase and struggle with our differences is toxic. Sabrina wants us to learn her neophyte incantation 'We are all the same underneath'. Piss off.

2. Talk Radio. There is freedom of speech and then there's just old arseholes crapping on about the sales tax on cream sherry. How can one pretend to Voltaire's avowed purity and tolerate, much less defend, the right of a former Queensland broadcaster to fulminate to an HIV-positive caller, 'You're just using HIV as some kind of excuse ... you are a sick individual and I hope you just, ah, die horribly. Good evening.' Well, if there is also to be voluble soft-left, prissily postmodern pronouncements made by the likes of your author, I suppose we have to preserve, nay cherish, his right to be a thorough ring. Complaining direct to

these incontinent juggernauts or to their program managers merely bolsters their righteousness. I would read the antivilification legislation in your state or territory and then inform the Australian Broadcasting Authority or the Anti-Discrimination Board if you believe that the legislation has been exceeded. Then, give yourself an elephant stamp and a scrummy pony poster for your efforts. And remember, Granny is probably borrowing her politics from John 'Resuscitate The Nightmare' Laws. So you'd be wise to buy her some of Althusser's structuralist socialism next birthday.

3. *Friends*. I don't care how thin Courtney Cox is, how do those rancorous but peachy white kids afford the rent on a Manhattan apartment? Some forlorn raconteur decided that the dialogue was 'terse, snappy and chic' (rather like a spoiled chow-chow) and, lo the ersatz 'cult' status of *Friends* was synthesised. Damn journalist wannabes. Further, how does Lisa Kudrow's feebly erratic Phoebe fit into even the outrageously hyperreal model of situation comedy. All that past-life, rebirthing and dolphin deity nonsense would try the most vapid Sleek Twenty-something? And what is Matthew Perry? Try as I might, I cannot adequately pinpoint his comic function. He is so relentlessly average. He does not even evince the same quirky pulchritude as David Schwimmer. He's plain! I must commend the Friends solidarity, however. I am profoundly awed by their contractual demands. Not only is a New York stylist flown in to the LA studio to dress their fab locks, but they have demanded $100,000 US for each invidious episode and have bargained for syndication rights. Obviously, they are humble enough to read their own expiration dates.

4. 'Men's' Magazines. I've got no real problem with blokes' tacky stick mags. Mercifully, the buyer of *Hustler* intones

by his choice, 'My sex-life is poor and I've run out of fantasies so I'm taking this porno mag home to assist me in enjoying a vigorous wank!' At the time of writing, however, there are two locally produced factitious periodicals on the market that borrow shamelessly and ineptly from the mission statement of British rag *Loaded: For Men Who Should Know Better*. These magazines, I assert, form the literary equivalent of The Governors Pleasure and assorted lunchtime lingerie revues. The deluded client is treated to a magniloquent 'businessman's' greeting. Unlike the unaffected working man who simply visits an arcadian strip joint if he wants a healthy tug, the middle-class gent seeks something from a lingerie revue that is infinitely more wretched, pitiable and perverse than sexual gratification. He wants to feel important. He is in pursuit of 'executive' porn. He not only seeks affirmation of his virility but an assurance that he is in possession of refinement. It is infinitely more 'refined', I conjecture, to jerk yourself stupid to an uncalculated edition of *Screw* than to get excited by semi-nude pictures of Melissa Tkautz merely because there's an interview with Mystic Logician Edward de Bono on the next page. Nothing is more pathetic than a pretentious, rueful wanker. My only happiness is derived from the secure knowledge that such magazines will be struck by commercial failure. If you want tractable tits to ogle, you buy *Jugs*. If you want to pursue orthodox male leisure activities, you would sensibly procure *Field and Stream*. If you are one of the mercifully minuscule male minority that remains bereft of a workable self-image, I guess that you could ponder subscribing to either *Max* or *Ralph*.

5. Jana Wendt. Good on ya, Jana, for making Channel Nine pay to send you to uni for a year so you could do some post-grad linguistics work. Good on ya, Jana, for taking Channel Seven to court. But, excuse me, did I doze off for the millisecond

in which you emerged as the valiant antipodean saviour of impartial television reportage? Oh, so it was you who personally discovered that the police framed Tim Anderson? It wasn't *Four Corners* at all who first publicly addressed the execrable pheno-menon now referred to as the Stolen Children tragedy. No, it was Jana Reconciliation, Treaty, Stick With Wik, I Spend All My Spare Time Hangin' With Brother Noel At Cape York Land Council Meetings Wendt. That would be the same Jana who used her popularity as a platform to campaign against the hundreds of unnecessary hysterectomies performed on Australian women each year. Oh, silly me! Different Jana! You'd be the Jana who sat at the helm of *A Current Affair* promoting intrusive, biased, foot-in-the-door journalism? You'd be that other Jana, the one famous for her frothy, seductive celebrity interviews on *Sixty Minutes*. Fuck off. Not only are you responsible for making every female Australian journalist sound like a constipated milk-cow who is simply not in control of her faux-impassioned hoof movements, but you're a fucking rich hypocrite who has grown prosperous by reverently upholding orthodox company policy. No-one believes your Hallmark Of Quality bullshit.

6. *Consuming Passions*. I know his recipes are good. I just can't help it. The guy really shits me. No-one can be that happy about cooking. He's so robust and all tea-and-scones-like, if you catch my flimsily expressed intent. Perhaps my disdain only arises as a result of the ever-increasing interest I have in tenderised fussy little cooking programs. One millisecond I am snarling like a fashionably incorrigible harridan and the next I am exclaiming graciously, 'Well, I never would have thought to do THAT with offal! My, that's savoury, cheap *and* relatively low in saturated fats! Get me to a charcuterie of note!' I am sagely informed by astrologers, according to whom I have triple Cancer and a Virgo

ascendant, that I cannot outrun my cosmically ordained need to furtively nest. I, however, attribute my reluctant fascination with televised gastronomy to having far too much spare time on my hands.

7. 'Youth' Television. I refer to no single program. They're all unspeakably vile, overelaborate and hypercorrect. What happens to programmers when they're confronted by a teenaged demographic? They fall apart, employ the first emaciated 'wacky' boy with fudged hair, coordinated casuals and a pierced septum who walks in the door, and instruct the camera operators, 'Use only HIP AND NOW angles!' The bizarre and confusing fact remains: programs for toddlers are really rather good. *Play School*, *Bananas In Pyjamas* and *Sesame Street* are all brilliant. If I ever deigned to reproduce (however, I am convinced that my womb is poison) I'd probably even whack on the teev for *Romper Room* and *Here's Humphrey*. Why can we ably entertain a notoriously demanding nought to five demographic while we fail to edify the lives of adolescents? Perhaps the average pubescent citizen does not need to be engaged by the laboured, patently affected overuse of phrases such as 'heaps cool', 'filth' and 'sick'. With their HAPPENING ranting about drugs, safe sex and Heaps Cool Way Rad Filth Sick Sony play-station merchandise, they nauseate and insult youngsters who are, for the most part, quite adept conversationalists. Not only do such programs aimlessly brutalise popular phraseology, they appear didactic, sententious and most decidedly the antithesis of heaps good.

8. *Getaway*. First and foremost my concern is: no matter how many books I write I'll never be able to afford a tropical holiday in a Swiss-designed health spa and colonic irrigation treatment clinic. (I spend my life encumbered by ravenous jealousy). Why does Channel Nine persist in making me covet my

neighbour's tax return cheque? At least they temper reports of such elaborate retreats with appraisals of accursed family-oriented boot camps in the Whitsunday Islands, I suppose. Nothing makes me bristle so much as the joyous peal of childish laughter, the threat of buffet dining and communal aqua-aerobics lessons. The other thing is THAT WOMAN AND BOTH OF HER TWO AMPLE UMBER NONPOROUS BOUNCING BREASTS. Yes, after many episodes featuring your cleavage in the foreground, we are sufficiently aware that you have an all-over camel bisque tan. We know that you have sorrel-brown perfectly fashioned boozies that arrive at exotic locations hours before you and your matching luggage. We suspect that an order of cosmeticians has been engaged by you lest your luxuriant caramel fun-bags are deprived temporarily of their enviable Sienna luminescence. We are positive that you employ a nipple wrangler to erect your cupreous aureole. Now, please, just put them udders away.

9. Fairfax newspapers. Now, where do these people get off pretending to be the guardians of decent impartiality in the Australian media landscape? For a start, they put me on the front page of their stinking tabloid when I was busted for cannabis possession. This is despite my assertion to a very reasonable Downing Centre magistrate via my very reasonable lawyer that I had no wish to publicly romanticise the fact of my flagrantly pathetic and irresponsible use of the prohibited narcotic. (Gasp! I actually do think that pot rots your brain and precludes the possibility of you producing anything useful. It is an interval in my life that I shall not revisit.) Anyhow, they smeared a very unflattering photograph of me beside a headline that ran TRIPLE J STAR DRUGS. I didn't mind the 'star' reference. Beyond that, however, the article provided nothing but mucky speculation

about my moral fibre and continued employment by the ABC. They even contacted a Coalition politician notorious for disdaining my network. Just to help them bring it up in parliamentary question time, I gather. Thanks, oh impartial and elite bastion of pure journalism. Patently, I have profoundly personal reasons for cancelling my subscription to the *Sydney Morning Herald*. I just wish they'd stop being so piss-elegant about how Murdoch doesn't own them and how crap News Limited is and settle down to the business of writing quality news.

10. *Entertainment Tonight*. I hate myself for adoring it so. I hate that I have to wait up until 3 a.m. to enjoy it. Of course, it was never that effortlessly slippery and edible after John Tesh left to become a New Age ambient pianist. I love John Tesh! I want to be the confidante of the personable Mary Hart! Why am I so compelled to devour the details of Ted Danson's new hair transplant, Johnny Depp's most recent tattoo and Tom Cruise's victimless good fucking humour? Do I really care that Mia has adopted ten new orphans, that Winona has donned yet another ill-fitting crinoline for a Merchant-Ivory US rip-off or that Farrah has agreed to a further series of gyneacologically intrusive shots of her fifty year old pudenda? Apparently, I do care. I can't get enough. Give me more more more unsubstantiated salacious celebrity gossip. What is the shape and the texture and the origin of this insatiable yawning abyss in my bosom that cries to be filled with news of the misfortune of others more beautiful than I? Buggered if I know.

11. Yahoo web-based chat rooms. These are the only rooms I can get into at work. Damn that repressive firewall. The Yahoo censor changes expletives to @#$%* and the extremely useful word 'shit' to 'poop'. I told somebody in Oslo that they were shitting me and it printed 'Bastard25 says: Sexy_Nordic_Guy_27,

stop talking about your @#$%*ing sad @#$%* you are poopting me!' And then 'Sexy_Nordic_Guy_27 is IAC @#$%*ing with his massive blonde @#$%* IRL and cyber @#$%*ing Bastard25's digital @#$%*. LOL. AFC.' Obviously such prim censorious applications make decent conversation impossible. Some of us have real swearing needs. However, now that I'm finally online at home, I am yet to find a chat room appropriate to my criteria. It's all, Have you got big bosoms? and Do you like Alanis She's Not Really That Ironic Morissette?

12. The Lifestyle Channel. When I agreed to the evil cable purveyor, the fiendishly affable young salesperson assured me that as I had nominated a passing interest in the Beaux Arts on my application form that I would adore this service. I had assumed that the Lifestyle Channel would provide me with wall-to-wall nonstop repeats of the Antique Road Show. I adore the simpering avarice of this program. 'So how much do you think my tinder-box is worth, Jonathan?' Slaver, pant, expectant intake of breath. I had premonitions of Sister Wendy on an apologetic Crusader Sites tour, her little wimple troubled by the gusts that whip about the awe-inspiring Crac de Chevalier, her endearing speech imped-iment echoing around Halikarnossis as she stormed the imposing fortification at Bodrum, her fervently religious eyes upturned as she paid homage at Ephesus, a beautifully preserved Doric master-piece and the last reputed residence and final resting place of the Blessed Virgin. I was also hoping for some interesting programs about sex as I refuse to pay the extra $14.95 per month to pur-chase The Adult Channel. No. It's all home handy-person renov-ations, tiny dogs and unworthy toddlers' transactional analysis.

13. *Beverly Hills 90210*. As someone who worshipfully thanks Aaron Spelling for his laudable contributions to western popular culture on an almost daily basis, I am displeased to admit

that he seems unable to dispose of this millstone. I can only assume that its continued existence is based on the fact of it remaining a vehicle for his daughter Tori, the still virginal Donna, and his creepy son whose name eludes me at present. To paraphrase Kenny 'The Gambler' Rogers, you've gotta know when to hold 'em, know when to fold 'em, know when to walk away and know when to run. (Advice Kenneth should probably himself have heeded when brave animal liberationists dressed in rooster costumes cluckingly picketed his umpteenth wedding for reported cruelty to the chickens he persists in roasting at his now famous chain of family poultry restaurants). As far as my influence extends, I think the show should have gone into permanent recess on the day that Brenda left. The reportedly inebriated antics of this unstuck young Republican cutie-pie doubtless motivated the creative complexity that was Brenda Walsh. She was so authentic-ally self-absorbed, spiteful, ideologically corrupt and gorgeous. Exactly what one would expect from a WASP Beverly Hills Princess. Regardless of the squishy liberal, loving, reasonable and just ministrations of Ma and Pa Walsh, Brenda remained reso-lutely rotten. Valerie, her unconvincingly curvaceous replacement, is portrayed as a victim. Valerie is only a Kelly-hating bitch because circumstances have conspired against her. Fuck under-standing, Aaron. That's not what made you rich. We were not expected to empathise with Joan Collins's Formaldehyde Alexis nor with Heather Locklear's lo-carb Amanda nor with the overtly sensual postbellum belle-fatale of the Southern-themed *Savannah*, Peyton. Bring back Brenda, because every day is Brenda day and many of us lived merely to loathe her.

14. The fact that I have to pay hard won cash to see *Larry Sanders*. *Larry Sanders* is, quite simply, the greatest sitcom ever contrived. Gary Shandling, the show's star and creator, is an

unmitigated evil genius. Exquisite and inviolate as it is, I resent having to proffer $49.95 each month to enjoy it. Such bitter resentment should be freely available to all who seek and require it. If you have not yet revelled in its perfidiously cold, soulless wonder, I suggest that you do so immediately. Rip Torn is stupendously unctuous as a hardened late-night show executive producer, ego wrangler and as a man fully consumed by the pernicious demands of an aggrieved network. Hank Kingsley, the rueful late-night sidekick, is perhaps comedy's most obnoxious, tragic and self-serving creation since something that Aristophanes probably wrote or *Rhoda*'s Carlton The Doorman. Hank is even more contemptible, spineless and rapacious than *Seinfeld*'s George Castanza. Larry is a prunelike, egoistic B-list late-night talk-show host and habitual divorcee who, on occasion, is legitimately funny. The defective, cynical production contretemps evinced within *Larry Sanders* make those kids at *Frontline* appear sanitised by contrast. *Larry Sanders* convincingly asserts that there is no good remaining within the entertainmnt milieu.

15. *Dolly* Magazine. When I speak with girlish youngsters, and these occasions are not rare, I find them excitedly engaged in the production of cyberzines, Slap Up A Spice Girl CD-ROMs and overtly feminist virago caterwauling above frenetic guitar and wildly careening drum patterns. I hear them discussing the misogyny inherent in contemporary music. I see them pasting eyes over the vicinity of their nipples on T-shirts so that men may no longer objectify women's breasts unimpeded. I giddily reverberate to the industrial-strength crush of their walking boots upon urban pavements. At twenty-nine I rejoice that my young sisters have extended the promise offered in turn to me by my revolutionary fearless feminist foremothers. Great, I surmise, I can relax and have an alpha-hydroxy facial peel now. There is a batallion of

impertinently youthful, unapologetically loose and ebullient babes to continue my life's work. This is the closest I will ever come to an unparralleled, seamless maternity. So what's up with *Dolly* magazine and its coy appreciation and euphemistic appraisal of the fabulous things that young women now confidently do? Has the Packer family got something against us dirty loud-mouthed lascivious stop-outs?

16. Parenthood columnists. All the grandiose major broadsheets feature such mawkish nonsense in their weekend editions. Do we care that the sociopathic Brandon had a rare softball victory, moving hs normally stalwart, always prolix, journalist father to shed sizable masculine tears? Do we give a shit about the peculiar tensions that arise in the mornngs of a chic yummy mummy who has to balance her talk-show commitments and her dramaturg's contract with the challenge of preparing a nutritionally equitable packed lunch? Would we risk our lives to save Jacinta from her burning Woollahra demi-mansion simply because her caring, neo-parenting pater eulogised the premature death by strangulation of her guinea pig called Demeter in a national daily newspaper? Would we offer Alexander one of our spare internal organs just because he wrote his subliterate mummy a touching and promsing haiku relating his recent experience of dead-legging the hall monitor? Would we attend the birthday tea of the pathologically acquisitive Allegra because we were profoundly moved by her male progenitor's account of how she turned her architect uncle's Frank Lloyd Wright original draft into a fascinating mosaic? No, of course we wouldn't. Children are only interesting if they're related to you by blood or you're a professional behaviourist. It is not that I despise children, by any means. I admire their apparent cranial resilience when they head-butt mahogany furniture and I revere the soft three ply absorbency of their minds

and if I ever get a kid on loan, I intend to read it *The Trial* by Franz Kafka at bedtime just so it doesn't get any ideas about the world being a nice place. Moreover, I do fret for the future mental health of these poor lambs. Toilet training, the acquisition of linguistic skills and the Oedipal phase are all traumatic enough without some qrandiloquent, prideful parent comically document- ing these watershed transitions for consumption by a national audience. When I developed my first filament of underarm hair, I cut it off with nail scissors and swore my mother to secrecy upon pain of death. If she had told anyone, much less a bals- amic vinegar free-basing double-income haute-bourgeois constituency, I'd be more disturbed than I already am. These people are in covert league with the Australian Association For Psychology.

17. In-flight audiovisual entertainment. First, the cattle class headphones are uncomfortably substandard and the sound they emit is of marginally worse quality than a low-wattage battery-operated AM transistor radio held up to the mouthpiece on an old bakelite phone via dirty low bandwidth landlines and received by me somewhere in the vicinity of Mt Isa. Second, they're barely worth stealing and if you do nick them you then have to go to Radio Shack to procure a diminishing attachment so they'll fit in your discman jack. Ultimately, however, what came out of them was bad in the first instance. Aloft air-time seems to be the exclusive province of those who have failed miser- ably as commercial radio jocks. As one of the many civilians who are prone to occasional fits of areonautical paranoia, I am neither soothed nor enraptured by the domestic airline who chooses to assault me with Richard Marx, Vivaldi's Four Fucking Margarine Ad Seasons and choice audio cuts from the putatively funny Hyacinth Bucket in *Keeping Up Appearances*. As for the tele-

vision, well it's more sanitised than Yahoo chat rooms. Any potentially interesting viewing is punitively cut to incomprehensible nonsequitous ribbons with the template provided by that nebulous, all-purpose rationale, Community Standards. The only potential in-flight entertainment lies in watching strangers attempt entry to the mile high club, trying to guess what consists in your 'meal' and observing terse relationships fall silently apart in the air.

18. Ray Martin. Without whom no such list would be complete. All right, so he attends the occasional Walking Together reconciliation committee meeting. Up you go, little Ray. And he did, eventually, stick it right up Pauline Hanson. Not a trying task, I'd warrant, but up you go, Ray, in any case. I must impart, if I were to spend eternal perdition in the company of a present or former Channel Nine employee, I'd choose the hapless Ray over the glossy Jana every time. However, there is no available means of excusing *A Current Affair*'s relentless pursuit of the poor Paxton family. For scurrilous weeks on end the Paxtons functioned to assuage middle Australia's doubt that mass unemployment AND the national deficit were both, quite simply, nothing more than the by-products of the laziness evinced by three long-hairs in outer suburban Melbourne. Heavens. This country's fiscal uncertainty could have nothing to do with global economics or federal government mismanagement. Absolutely not. Propelled by this ethos, *A Current Affair* was perfectly entitled to display Bindi Paxton in an immodest cream bikini on at least three separate occasions. The little minx deserved such mass objectification. She was, after all, living far beyond squalor entirely at your expense. There was also the case of the electronics technician in Sydney's Rozelle who took his own life after another fearless exposé by *A Current Affair*. It must have been a frus-

tratingly sluggish news week when they decided to reveal the awful truth: tradespeople charge you much more than the cost of their raw materials. Well, duh. As the daughter of a builder, I have long been familiar with tradies. None of them, to my knowledge, reside in palaces. Furthermore, they spend three to four years subsisting on a miserly journeyman's stipend in order to hone their craft. Tradies are, for the most part, damn dexterous folk who reinvent my television, reseal my drainpipes, erase my radial fractures and generally perform tasks that the lay person simply cannot. I am glad that they exist and that the blokes amongst them still wear nice little King Gees. Finally, this dead guy had been granted a scholarship by a major electronics consortium, so he couldn't have been that shit. Ray persists in purveying his wide-eyed, amenable superhero brio. I wish he'd just stop pretending to be such a reasonable, squishy man.

19. People at the railway station who persist in guilt-tripping me to buy their heinous lefty sook rags. When they wanly intone *Socialist Worker, Green Left* or *Pinko Review,* I find myself uncomfortably conflicted. If I don't buy the damn thing, will they think me a renegade, reactionary fifth columnist who seeks to thwart the promise of the people's revolution? Will they slander me as soon as I depart the platform, imagining that I have given birth to two private-school-attending caucasian children, that I play bridge and inhabit a cosy owner-occupied bunker in Balmain? More to the point, do I even care what these nascent apparatchiks are saying about me once I have vanished? Do I mind that they hiss 'Oppressor!' and envisage my life as an emolliated nonchalant two-step performed about supple abundantly padded Laura Ashley print incidental furnishings? Well, I do mind a bit, as it happens. I go to residents for reconciliation meetings. On occassion, I address the Young Labor left. Hey, I still march

on International Women's Day. The only means of demonstrating the intensity of my soft-centred left passion is to agree to purchase the damn publication. Or so I presume. I proffer my two dollar coin, and they behold me with silky condescension as they sub-vocalise, 'Poor pliant class traitor, she's wearing Mystere by Rochas. Not only is it French and a shit-load more expensive than patchouli essence, it is redolent of the acquisitive commodity-fetishistic eighties. At least the poor dear is making an effort, I suppose. Shall I ask her to a meeting?' Then they use my money to fund the befuddlement and unbracing of the soft heads of callow first year university students. Which will, in turn, produce more *Green Left* vendors, thereby increasing the risk to me of regular anxiety as I board the train. Best just to scream, 'Leave me alone, smelly leftie,' and hurriedly walk on.

20. *Animal Hospital*. Yet another repugnant, mawkish proponent of 'reality TV' programming to which I am unwillingly drawn and by which I am perfervidly affected. Oh, those poor solemn pussy cats and lugubrious brave itty-bitty puppy dogs. How can I afford such hypocrisy? I am an eager carnage munch-ing omnivore, I choose to remain active within the rapacious and fluffy animal despising free market economy and I have not volunteered my services to the RSPCA for some years. Yet I weep tender tears whenever I subject myself to this ardent melodrama. You know, I've been quietly and profoundly requiring the services of a neural surgeon for some time lest my wisdom teeth impact further into my head at calcified speed. I risk, I am sure, with such medical negligence, the bloody, suppurating and hellish emergence of a tooth sized cranial fissure that will decimate my faculty for independent thought and probably result in my employment by Channel Nine. Apart from the fact that she's always very insolent about my oral high-jinks and she charges like

a bull who has recently undergone intricate root canal surgery, why do I persist in avoiding my umbrageous orthodontist? Particularly when I fitfully consider sending money to the producers of *Animal Hospital* to save the tail mobility of a stray tabby cat.

CHAPTER NINE
INTIMATE RELATIONSHIPS AND HOW TO AVOID THEM

Participation in a loving, caring, reciprocal and complementary adult relationship is evidence of one's spiritual growth. Yeah, fucking right. This is what most manuals of self-esteem would have you believe. If you're not yet engaged in a tentative, non-querulous and punctilious sexual partnership, then you're an unmitigated junk heap. And you've probably got halitosis as well.

When affronted by such twee and virtuous unravelment, I am not certain where to locate my first offensive blow. Possibly a lower adbominal assault upon the myth of complementarity would be circumspect. We have briefly engaged in the dissection of this lie in our discussion regarding gender travesty and recommended identity transvestism. This dichotomous approach to life and human being and endeavour, as previously asserted, forms the basis of our current notional western model. A system of thought that is founded upon the template of binary opposition will necesarily privilege the One and subjugate the Other. Black is a pale privation of white, remarkable only for the One which it is not. Black is defined purely in terms of its absence of whiteness.

There is no black-specificity. Black is simply understood as a lack of whiteness. Some other antithetical pairings include: Good and Evil, Fact and Fiction, Literal and Figurative, Philosophy and Literature, Purity and Corruption, Man and Woman, Coke and Pepsi. The one does not stir, breathe or exist without the other. There are, of course, anomalies. The tenants of such an unreasonable dichotomous edifice are bound to ocassionally exceed the terms of their unreasonable lease. Many of us, for example, are frightfully epicene. We commonly possess both male and female characteristics. Friedrich Nietzsche's rich text *Thus Spoke Zarathustra* similarly refuses the paradigms of either philosophy or literature. The critique that greeted this publication, along with his reputed syphilis, is probably what drove him around the bend. Folks tend to adore compliance and so they embrace binary order with ardour. Opposing or complementary pairs are nice and easy to read. We do not like to be confused. We spurn the woman who is raffish and loud. This is possibly why Ding Dong no longer works on *Hey! Hey! It's Saturday*. We also refuse the text that is writerly and that encourages rigorous interpretation. James Joyce (no, not the bloke who works for a newspaper) once proclaimed that he had spent twenty years forging the convoluted polyglot that is *Finnegan's Wake*. He expects us to set aside twenty more to read it. (Joyce is a writerly modernist in the extreme, though, and buggered if I'm going to risk comsummate insanity just so I can boast at genteel dinner parties.) I looked at the first page of *Finnegan's Wake* once. Sadly Joyce is subventing way too many boundaries at once for me to want to even go near him ever again. I digress. (Well again, knock me over with the Cliff's crib notes for *Portrait Of The Artist As A Young Fucking Man*.) We shall return to relationships.

Okay. So complementarity is crap. We are not restless

halves eternally yearning to be made whole. At the very best, we can hope to find a partner with a comfy genital configuration, decent oral hygiene and the kindness to make us a toasted cheese sandwich when we're apoplectic with occupationally inspired rage. Let go of the florid bilious mystic hippie shit and think yourself honoured if you're getting regular sex. No One can fulfil you, you forlorn waste-oid. Unhappily, it is left to you to address the means at your immediate disposal and subsequently auto-motivate the squishy old viscera from a dire grievous depression to a state of tenable unhappiness. If you're actually deliriously happy, then fret not, it won't last. The most you can ever hope for is a stable state of manageable misanthopy and self-loathing. There exists no karmically splendid individual who is equipped to galvanise your *werltschmetrz*. (Except maybe a really solid analyst.) Patently, people are able to make you feel crappy. I do not find them expedient, however, in improving the humour.

Some female readers may have encountered *The Rules*. This execrable and slim volume (addendum now available) recommends securing a partner at great personal cost. You're not allowed to have sex with your intended for THREE MONTHS for a start. You cannot accept a spontaneous invitation from a man lest he regards you as loose and accessible. You must lose weight and, on those rare occasions when trousers are permissible, you should don a brightly coloured snug-fitting top. You must be a 'Creature Unlike Any Other'. (I'm not sure what this means. It's got something to do with shutting the fuck up and looking winsome, I think. I assume that it has nothing whatsoever to do with genetic engineering.) You must grow your hair and perform regular, rigorous pedicures. You must not drink to excess. (I actually thought that this was sound advice until I discovered that they meant stop at one chablis spritzer. Twenty schooners constitutes excess in my drinking realm.) You must rehearse speaking mellifluously. Never suggest sex or detail the connubial techniques which may give you pleasure. You must never initiate contact with a man and, importantly, you must only return one third of his calls. Apply cosmetics scantily and with muted taupe finesse. In essence, don't do squat, get thin, stay off the piss, buy some fuchsia frocks and pretend that you find sex distasteful. Needless to impart, this poorly formulated and deeply duplicitous manifesto, which makes the *Women's Weekly*'s home hints page read like Andrea Dworkin by contrast, went on to sell millions of copies worldwide. Well, fuck me, what won't some people spend their working dollar on? I swear if I marketed Cat Turd In A Box some dotard would buy it with the hope of detonating her cellulite.

In any case, the thrust of my argument is, FUCK OFF. What the hell are they thinking? Is it desirable to spend an eternity in crushing, weight controlled servitude to some moron who was stupid enough to choke on your flimsy scam? Do you really think you'll be sated by a supine life of motionless sex, diluted white wine and brash Versace ripoffs? What if you feel like shaving your head one day, you stupid bint? Will your ill-devised conceptual locale then implode? Will you immediately lose your enraptured husband, gain fifty kilos and fill your pez dispenser with a random mixture of xanax, lithium and heroin? And what of your tortured mate? Perhaps he was propelled toward you in the first instance because he slyly glimpsed you in your element. Tube skirt up near your runny eyelashes revealing roseaceous faux-lace slatternly underwear as you athletically entertain your coven on a tabletop while unsteadily performing a *Knees Up Mother Brown/ Rip Her To Shreds/Doll Parts* medley between onanistic gesticulations, womanly gulps of OP rum and tokes on a Churchill cigar.

That, to many men of my acquaintance, is the very picture of desirable femininity unbound.

Men, of course, appear not to have the same overt obsession with contented coupledom. At least I assumed that this was the case until I commenced my attendance at singles' tea dances, encounter groups and seminars in the course of my research for this book. The poor darlings appear to be similarly entrapped by the fey promise which insists that loving reciprocity is the logical endpoint of all human endeavour. Thousands of them flock to these prosaic lecture-cum-pick up joints with alacrity. And not all of them, seemingly, are dribbling losers complete with moist copies of JRR Tolkien middle-earth texts in the back pockets of the tea and urine stained boilersuits in which they are disturbingly clad. Of course, you get your one or two average sociopaths who have pictures in their goretex, velcro snap wallets of their mothers with the words 'Die slut' scrawled across them in scarlet ink. However, these uneasy gentlemen are a doddle to spot because they are the ones who sit outside the ladies' rest room for the duration of the stultifying sermon, only to arise to sniff the musky seat of a chair that has recently been vacated by a warm female parishoner. Seriously, however, most of the blokes seem relatively sane, if just a little emotionally fortuneless.

It troubles me that men and women gracelessly stalk the corridors of our social economy looking so damn needy. An unforgivably expensive feng shui home renovation, a palette of quality Swiss dark chocolate bitter truffle balls or a savage rolfing are just as likely to obfuscate doubt as a steady partner. I have an acquaintance who regularly and expertly details this unblinking quest for satisfaction. 'What is The Thing?' she will often demand of the air. She continues her one-woman interrogation until symbolic order is bullied into offering her a reply. The Thing has manifested as the *Die Hard* video trilogy, a framed wedding photo of Princess Grace, a chemically distended Tupperware party in the company of her lewdest comrades, a nude male maid, a diffident and diffuse same-sex encounter, origami lessons, a new stratocaster, a large posy of red tulips, a dental appointment, shiatsu massage, a koi carp for her paddling pool (itself a former Thing), Mexican home delivery, chiropractic, anchovies, a victorian paperweight, Buddhism-lite, the Rolling Stones song book, a bottle of shiraz and a wank. Much of the latter. I have always envied the well-charted topography of her desire. She is fully apprised of the character of her meandering will. All her wishes, she acknowledges, are consanguineous. The desire for soy-based eggnog, for example, has the same origin and lineage as the desire for a perfect partner. One should not encumber one's self, she sagely postulates, with a mortgage, the potential woes of another and another's potentially woeful CD collection when a trip to the pub may suffice.

This is not to surmise, of course, that all relationships are ultimately fruitless, expensive and deleterious to the health of one's affective pulse. Such extrapolation would constitute big-booted, doctrinaire, no-fun ugly feminism. And I have given up big-booted, doctrinaire, no-fun ugly feminism for Lent. I will simply conjecture that a great number of suppositionally 'loving' relationships are formed on the basis of coveting The Thing. Many individuals go 'steady', get married, produce ungainly children, have arguments about decor and proffer their souls to financial institutions when all they were really required to do was perform a number of discrete self-serving acts. The divorce rate would not be so stupendously high if people would just buy themselves a jar of cocktail onions when they felt like it. Frequent and cautious self-indulgence is a whole fuck-load cheaper than a wedding, damn it! (Yes, fuck-load is a technical term.) If you genuinely feel that you are substandardly sutured, potholed and incomplete, then stitch yourself up, gorge until you are sick and reinvent yourself with regular treats. The wilful sussurations of your desire to be 'whole' can and must be silenced before you go running headlong into partnership. If you're that fucking needful and tortured by gaping runny passional sores, you are in no state at all to begin life in the constant company of another. If you constantly demand of another that he or she express the histrionic pus from your disgusting self-inflicted wounds, they'll eventually dash screaming in abject terror taking the rhapsodical cure-all Savlon with them when they judiciously leave. This is why *The Rules* are not pragmatic, ladies. If you prissily jog about the gendered world NEEDING a husband, DEMANDING fulfilment and generally expanding that synthetic chasm in your (prettily exposed) breast that demands penetration by another, you're just going to end up sucking percodan smoothies through a bendy hospital straw. Poor deluded blokes. They've got their own convoluted shit to deal with. They don't need you banging on about complementarity, reciprocity and holes that require immediate multipronged invasion. Become impenetrable, actively pursue The Thing and sternly remind yourself that it's only wussy-chicks who borrow and employ pop-femme parlance like 'My Aching Need'. Burn those Rules and embrace your ugliest eccentricities with elan.

And, gentlemen, although at present you do not face an insurmountable hill of torrid and touchy text as testimony to your 'need' for a sympathetic spouse, I am aware that a number of you are equally corrupted by the ideal of Healing Love. As women primp, reshape and reduce themselves, men also modify their physiques and demeanour in an effort to magnify their chick-magnetism. I have tacitly observed male flatmates squeeze themselves into exiguous leather pants. I have witnessed their solarium and Nautilus-machine bound struggles to change from pale compelling and delicate minikins into hulking, bullocky, bronzed Leviathans. I have seen them fashion unforgivable poetry, endure unthinkable fibrous diets and, most pathetically, pretend to be able to play the guitar. (NB: Gents! Unless you are truly musically gifted, abandon this stochastic procedure at once. Women are not so thick and devoid of discernment as to be seduced by atonal, frowzy versions of 'Sitting On The Dock Of The Bay'. They will NOT deem you to be bewitching bluesy blades. They will simply tell their friends what a thorough dick you are.) The conscious desire to function as a desirable object is, perhaps, not in itself overwhelmingly irksome. (That is unless, of course, the gentleman concerned utilises the Lynx Java range of Scented Toiletries For Men to perfect his appeal. Such an olfactory affront pleases no-one.) However, the desire to transform your especial strangeness or waywardness into a cheap, cheerful and marketable bland commodity aimed at the lowest common marriageable denominator is both unprincipled and wanton. Such a profane attempt to engage the affections of a debauched and complacent unreconstructed mass constituency at the cost of one's more intriguing parts should possibly be referred to as the *Hey! Hey! It's Saturday* Syndrome. You silence and sever ties with Ossie the pink oracular Ostrich (or the dark, teeming and prescient id), you sexualise, discredit and fire the bosomy female comedian (the sensible, functional and robust ego) and then proceed to spend several years in the top twenty and on the christmas card database of Jamie Packer (the censorious, proper and repressive superego) dysfunctionally making fun of poofters and plump little kids. You occasionally wake screaming, only to be soothed by the weight of your own account balance. The putrescent ooze from your every pore that evinces and decants your discontinued, complex past tests the skill of Channel Nine's most vigilant and industrial cosmeticians. Certainly you marry, perhaps three or four times. A pyrrhic victory, I suggest. Sometimes a Logie is no substitute for genuine pride. Just ask anyone on the quality shop floor at the award-unencumbered current affairs department of ABC television.

Men and women! Are you one of these pernicious people? Do you sit sedentary and forlorn in the hope that some mellifluous bearlike protaganist will leap into the trite pulp narrative your life has become and heroically attend to your wounds with the enviable skill of a private surgeon? It's just not going to happen. In a mere matter of days, your newest true love will discern just how abominably greedy you are. The harder you strive for perfection in your relationship, the more repulsive and objectionable you will become. You cannot maintain the fiction of your assiduous, unblinking calm. You have created a needy beast. The ding-a-ling identity you have attempted to repress has gone sour from lack of maintenance and now threatens to seep and discolour your every exchange. You are a needy fuckwit. Are you one of these avaricious swine? Take this simple test, please.

HELEN'S NEVER FAIL FIVE POINT AM I A NEEDY FUCKWIT TEST

1

Your new fluffy cosset does not appear motivated when you whinge loudly of irritable bowel aerobatics and demand Mylanta or similar palliative. There's none in the house. Do you:

(a) feel like a bit of a prune for griping in the first

instance, drink some chocolate milk and proceed to ignore the minor abdominal discomfort;

(b) quietly intone to yourself, 'Well he/she's a bit of a dick. Well I suppose they MIGHT be tired' and semistorm out of the house to the pharmacy, returning with a spanky treat lest you have offended your intended;

(c) bang on endlessly about your Candida-propelled syndrome, launch into a prolonged and infantile 'nobody fucken understands my pain' treatise and threaten to take your own life via means of laxative abuse if he/she does not immediately engage the services of a reputable chemist?

2

Your recently acquired delicious inseparable wants to go and see Sidewinder while you have already silently formed plans to endure the new poncy Peter Greenaway film. Do you:

(a) think, 'Shit! I'm glad I didn't tell him/her I wanted to go and see a dreadful art wank opus made by that artless Pom turd. Sidewinder sounds like a much better idea';

(b) indecorously and affectedly jut out your lower lip and say, 'Ooow! But I wanted to go to the movies,' then immediately confronting your guilt, express your belief that Sidewinder is a top band which embraces psychedelia with learned aplomb and that Peter Greenaway came to postmodernism way too late and ineffectively in life and that if the offer still applied, yes, you'd love to go. Besides which, only a handful of tenacious art geeks with green fudge spiky hairdos, cosmetic nerd glasses and trust funds will make it to the cinema to wrestle with this century's bombastic filmic equivalent of the irksome Wagner. So it'll be straight to video in a month. And art cinema seats are so damn uncomfortable;

(c) accuse your betrothed of being a facile, crude, disingenuous, prosaic, underclass imbecile. Inform them sternly that not only are you aghast at the poor standard of their leisure time inclinations but you are also mortally offended that your needs are being ignored AGAIN?

3

You have recently commenced a cohabiting arrangement with your new sex toy. He or she wishes to ritually signify the demise of his/her freedom by listening to *Led Zeppelin Four* repeatedly and doing bucket bongs in the lounge room with a couple of mates. You find the prospect of sleep unlikely. Do you:

(a) leap out of bed and race toward the revelry, pausing only at the looking glass to ensure that your reflection conveys fetching dishevelment. Scream, 'Give Us A Billy, Sex Dog!', consume your weight in cannabis and shake your head in baggy appraisal to 'Black Dog', completely forgetting that you were ever tired;

(b) tentatively move toward the soiree with the intention of asking all gathered to keep it down. After a partially expressed admonishment, become mesmerised by 'Going To California', murmur, 'Fuck that Jimmy Page can play' and on in act of homage to both Led Zeppelin's west-coast subculture posturing and your beloved's diminished liberty, partake in just enough wacky tebacky to send you off to slumberville;

(c) storm righteously from your floral print flannelette sheets resplendent in your rage and baby doll nightie/striped shortie pyjamas and wail about how you need sleep, acknowledgment, privacy, respect, solitude, love, regular colonic irrigation and a yobbo-free domicile. Totally defecate on the festive mood, openly chastise your partner and publicly admit to hating

Led Zeppelin. Brew a chamomile infusion as you coldly bid a farewell to the group of deflated stoner deadheads. Perform your nightly affirmations loudly with the secondary intention of keeping your sweetheart uncomfortably conscious for as long as possible?

4

You visit your special persona grata's house for the very first thrilling time. You note that she/he has a proclivity for porno. In fact, the X-rated videos are so numerous that it appears a new wing may have to be built to accommodate them. Do you:

(a) squeal, 'Oh, *Sodomania*! My Very Favourite!' and ask to borrow it after you have performed ebullient acts of open circum-clitoral or penile self-abuse on the shag pile in front of your beloved's sticky VCR;

(b) wonder if your new shadow is writing a dissertation on the evils of commodified erotica. Primly ask, 'Um, what do you use these for?' while indicating the gaudy heap of lascivious ferric oxide. When they unabashedly answer, 'To help me wank, silly' become curious, have a sly look at *Costa Rica Get-Away* and, during your next naked assignation, bravely attempt to duplicate the athletic enthusiasm of any of those involved in the poly-sexual, multiplayer interactive beach tableau;

(c) accuse your scrummy kitten of acceding to wholesale misogyny. Call them a pervert several times and start reciting fragments of Andrea Dworkin's repugnant, reprehensible and twisted text *Pornography*. Draw parallels between National Socialist Germany and *Soak My Tits In Cum*. Run away bawling and refuse to have any kind of sex that involves moaning?

5

Your nouveau/nouvelle amour suggests that you don an exceedingly transparent lace teddy/PVC nut-sack/bridle/nurse's uniform/several pots of blueberry conserve and a full can of Dairy Whip. You feel a tad uncomfortable about this request. Do you:

(a) chuckle wickedly and agree on the precondition that your bouncy boy or girl of the moment dresses in a Darrell Lea shop assistant's outfit and dutifully feeds you nougat Christmas pudding using only infrequently displayed body parts;

(b) titter nervously and agree to the indiscretion on the precondition that you get paid at least fifty bucks for your trouble. The cost of all accessories to be paid for by the client. You secretly videotape the event if he or she is a Coalition cabinet member;

(c) weep wretchedly, demand relationship counselling, repeat the request to your mother (and, conceivably, their own female progenitor and select sententious family members), buy some Prozac, be consoled by a papist official, write to Oprah, seek solace from any number of former primary school teachers and eventually accede to his/her suggestion on the precondition that you can document the indiscretion and later use it as a weapon for the term of your association then, secretly enjoy your dirty sticky subjugation, you moist hypocritical sicko?

Finished? Whacko! Please utilise Helen's Never Fail Five Point Am I A Needy Fuckwit Test Scoring Method:

Mostly As: Fuck, you're reasonable. A little too responsive, if you ask me. To employ parental rhetoric, if somebody asked you to put your head in the oven, you probably would. (If you are channelling Sylvia Plath at the time of reading, you are automatically exempt from this moot reprimand.) You have really pummelled the ideal of snivelling abetment into a portable little pigskin ball and run past the posts with it, haven't you? Buy yourself a nice present and get some help. There is something profoundly wrong with you and, doubt not, this relationship is doomed. Two miserly points. And you only got those because you like Led Zeppelin. I suggest that you undergo the Never Fail Five Point Am I A Meddlesome Overweening Dickhead Test post-haste.

Mostly Bs: You are one of those admirable and exotic creatures who is competently and impartially equipped to estimate his or her own level of comfort when it is posited in relation to the needs of another. You are fabulous and you should be mounted (frequently and expertly) and put on display in the National Gallery. Why aren't there more sensible people like you, you polysemous gorgeous accommodating but healthily self-interested Renaissance kind of girl or boy? One hundred points. Subtract ninety, because, patently, you fibbed. Ten points.

Mostly Cs: Who the fuck are you, you covetous, insatiable shit-head? You can barely operate the ring-pull on a tin of Heinz ham-enhanced spaghetti unaided, much less function adequately in a mature and stable adult partnership. You never really left university, did you? Your cloying undergraduate tendencies repulse just about everyone you meet. Your didactic demeanour, your fondness for hellishly bland alleged 'singer song-writers' such as the satanic Toni Childs, and your drab, reaction-ary, unforgiving mode of dress preclude the possibility of you ever being asked out to the football. How can you stand yourself, you meek, proselytising, judgemental, stinking anomaly? Lord knows, no-one else can abide you. Buy a stupid fucking fluffy cat called Deepak and feed it from your vast stock of herbal and pharma-ceutical angst remedies if you want to have anything approaching a fulfilling relationship. No partially sane, self-respecting human is capable of tending to the gargantuan forest of your aching, tangled demands. Nil, nada, donut, nothing. Anyone with as many Louise Hay books as you deserves naught but an enema, a Digestive biscuit and a good hard think. No points. One bonus point because you display great temerity in sifting through the ballistic tongue-lashing by the hapless, subacademic anti-Julie Burchill, Andrea Dworkin. Subtract half a point because you believe she constructed some really salient arguments in *Right Wing Women*. Half a point. And never bother me again.

If you are not one of those decadent souls who irresponsibly chases Romance in the hope that you will be saved, massaged and mended, you may very well belong to an equally repugnant order of wannabe brides and grooms. You may be one of those who aggressively and wilfully annuls an understanding of your own fervid demons in order that you may tend to the concerns of another. Any potential for personal enlargement is always volitionally constricted by your pathological ministrations to the pain of your parter. You could be the sort so mortified at the prospect of jousting with your own tireless idiocy that you fix your attention upon the shortcomings of some other silly limp fractious feeble-oid. Are you one of these execrable healers? You will be overjoyed to learn that I have, in my endearing and recently acquired gurulike idiom, prepared another Never Fail Five Point Test with which you may shortly measure your passive-aggressive pathos.

Before sharing with you the tumescent fruits of my tireless research and unswerving scholarly study, I believe it would be prudent for me to gingerly offer some canny advice and direction. I am qualified to do this because I have arisen as, of course, Miss

Anabolic Emotions of 1998. Oh, but I am the magnanimous Charity Queen. As you well know by now, I am the very quintessence of temperamental health. Yes, I am so charily together and I never allow ardent seepage. I would never, for example, opulently and publicly criticise one of my past occupational superiors as a cryptofascist sexist fuck-head resolutely unable to locate his bewizened member with the aid of a Maglite mine-strength industrial torch and two hoary hands. That was another silly girl who bore a striking resemblance to me. Possibly the same one who shortly thereafter forfeited her wage. And the very same psycho-femme who covertly confiscated her very reasonable and loving partner's Quake II CD-ROM because she wanted more attention. It wasn't me, which is why I am able to freely proffer such sterling advice regarding robust human relationships. Yes, I am free from any affective malady! Oh, bugger it. So I can provide no qualified exhortation to wellness. But Deepak Chopra is probably an intractable agoraphobic with a covert sugar abuse problem and his guileless barratry is just as shitty, if not more so, than mine. Okay, I am completely afflatus-deficient. I cannot muster my own awakening, so I probably have no hope of rousing you. Let's just complete the quiz, shall we?

HELEN'S NEVER FAIL FIVE POINT
AM I A MEDDLESOME OVERWEENING DICKHEAD TEST

1

Your luscious new minion is a student of ethnography. He or she is confronting great difficulty in tackling the concept of the Trobriand Islanders' system of exchange. This causes a little average friction between you. Do you:

(a) procure some rental games for the play-station, order a cheese crust pizza and resolve not to speak with your troubled partner until they have sufficiently scaled the concept of a gift-based economy. You get a little pissed at them for being so expansively thick and consumed while you are being so lavishly ignored. Doesn't this idiot know when they've got it so good;

(b) soothe and praise your flame for his or her academic valour, expediently skim read the primary texts, glance at the appropriate Learning And Culture bulletin boards on the world wide web and offer your services to engage in an impromptu ethnographical tutorial. You comically adorn the car with sea-shells before you pick him/her up from the library;

(c) enrol in a concentrated continuing education anthropology course of study at your own expense. You call your ducky's lecturer at home in an extravagant effort to grasp the nuances of the Kula Ring. You fundamentally marshal the linguistic structure of at least three Trobriand dialects and construct a helpful plywood diorama to scale. Eventually, you just write the essay yourself footnoting meticulously and offering the rash new hypothesis that Levi-Strauss was off his face on drugs?

2

You and your genial comrade are sharing your first knotless, tractable and contented winter season together. All is cosily unexacting until Possums begins to soggily wrestle with a virulent bout of kicking influenza. Do you:

(a) seek out a flu injection, imbibe an entire shrubbery's worth of pure echinacea, perniciously and punitively sterilise any household items that the diseased infidel may have potentially touched and burrow into a self-imposed quarantine refusing to see your poorly confidant, much less perfunctorily sup on their bodily fluids, until they can produce a doctor's certificate indicating fair and proper health. You are a little cranky about the inconvenience and you entertain the thought of embellishing your exile with a breathy call to a favoured ex-beau;

(b) ask around and find a semicompassionate doctor who favours vitamin therapy and procure your pet an immediate appointment. You thoughtfully buy your unwell beloved some Panadeine and horseradish tablets before stopping off at the gourmet deli to seize the internationally renowned antibiotic properties of wholesome chicken consomme. You lend him or her your folder-bound stockpile of *Vanity Fair* periodicals and cautiously leave them to their temporary misery;

(c) become aghast and apoplectic when you discover that your intended has not judiciously thought to invest in a comprehensive health plan. You consider committing acts of insurance fraud in between shoving an accurate-to-two-decimal-places rectal digital thermometer up their fundament every three minutes, forcing impossibly heaped dessertspoons of acrid and granular ascorbic acid down their flu ravaged throat and visiting multi-denominational temples to pray with secular abandon for their deliverance. In more extravagant moments, you imagine how pale, admirably strong and eloquent you will be at the remembrance service?

3

Your Close Personal Friend is acutely poisoned and demeaned by the rigours of his or her frantic work schedule. Do you:

(a) refuse to understand why anyone would even begin to address such occupational torment. You reprimand them for their immoderate egotism and sternly suggest that a smouldering, candlelit and costly encounter in which they function as primary choreographer and by which you benefit immensely may be the one true solution to their employment woes;

(b) candidly and volubly engage your dreamboat in a constructive and uplifting personal conference. You helpfully employ problem-solving techniques such as passional flow charts, impulsion pie graphs and incentive option trees where necessary. You quell your frenzied partner's truculence, induce him or her to arrive at a feasible understanding and then have really quality sex. You ebulliently assist your mate in comprehending this incident as a pathway to professional advancement rather than as an immutable obstruction;

(c) refer to your previously devised diagramatic data-base documenting the shape of your cosset's office politics and their immediate chain of command. You systematically call and abuse each criminal in the order of their sedition. You subscribe to several daily newpapers and ostentatiously leave the edited and highlighted Help Wanted lift-out in your fluffy's underwear drawer?

4

Your valued familiar is having an existential crisis. He or she frequently poses unwieldy epistemological questions such as 'Who Am I?', 'Why Do I Fucking Bother?' and 'Where Do All My Odd Socks Accummulate?' at inopportune moments. Do you:

(a) chastise your precious for their gross indulgence. You deter them from their project of unravelling the Telos and block their every move toward philosophical enlightenment. You hide their first edition of *Being And Nothingness*, expostulate ruefully and generally ban the topic or practice of phrenic doubt for all time. You make them purchase several new pairs of argyle-patterned socks;

(b) praise your prized possession for his or her inspired reductive errantry. You warmly state that such assiduous inquiry forms the basis for all that is decent in humankind. Together you disentangle weighty Sartrean concepts and joyously revel in your notional nausea. You commence a highbrow deconstructive correspondence slated for later publication. You have more quality sex. Importantly, you quash your egocentric suspicion that it is you, rather than the unknowable world, that propels your treasure to such acts of inquisitive attrition. Essentially, you transform what is apparently an insurmountable and enervating existential impasse into a happy, albeit fitful, opportunity for rosy debate and self-overcoming;

(c) refrain from offering remonstrance or sensible synoptic help and travel instead to the Druid New Age Book Emporium. Desperate to permeate the prickly surrounds of your beloved, doubting porcupine, you pierce their consternated membrane with the sabre of low-born solutions and pour nasty, allegedly cheerful hope into the crevise of their justified dissatisfaction. You buy them a gift voucher for a protracted series of EST seminars and wheel about them maniacally whistling 'Always Look On The Bright Side Of Life', 'On A Clear Day You Can See Forever', the theme from *The Bodyguard* and other menacingly chipper show tunes?

5

You have noticed that your amoroso fair has been enjoying the odd tipple. Well, as it happens, she or her has been devouring entire brewery conglomerates in a single night. As a consequence, you are enjoying only rare and overwhelmingly average connubial interludes and the quality of your relationship is suffering. Do you:

(a) dump the bastard. He or she was a dud bash anyway. You ensure that your dance card is full, acquire a becoming new hair-do and unhesitatingly propel youself into the arms, beds and orifices of a number of willing suitors. For good measure, you slash your ex-paramour's vestments, deposit liquid laxative into their gin and wilfully scrawl insults about the rest room walls of their preferred drinking establishment;

(b) strive to pinpoint the origin of your poppet's discontent. Reasonably and lucidly confront your adorable piss-artiste with the litany of your woes. Sensibly and moderately counsel your sloshed sweetheart and indicate the financial, emotional, mental and physiological detriment to their health such abandoned swigging threatens. Proffer documentary evidence as testimony to your remonstrance and valiantly hope that your puppy will perceive the error of his or her inebriated ways. If you are eventually defeated, you sadly depart and re-order your shattered life;

(c) employ *Party Of Five* as a primary model and imagine that your swinish dearie is just like Bailey Salinger. You follow Alcoholics Anonymous instructions to the letter and stage a histrionic intervention replete with battered empties, grandiose inspirational background music and a soiree of his or her disgruntled chums. You sing the serenity prayer loudly and repeatedly in the shower and employ phraseology such as 'Higher Power' on trips to the supermarket. Your life's work has become the salvation of some inebriated unworthy imp. You utilise the word 'recovery' at least fifty times a day and misplace any patience you may have formerly borne to those not currently engaged in a twelve step program?

Done? Fabulous! Avail yourself at once of Helen's Never Fail Five Point Am I A Meddlesome Overweening Dickhead Test Scoring Method:

Mostly As: My, we've got a robust little ego, haven't we? Isn't our true love just so lucky to attain an audience with us at all? How can one mere mortal be so desirable, urbane and effectively perfect? Well, I don't know! Listen here, you perverse, egomaniacal, faux-regal brat, NO-ONE is that prissy and special. To appropriate the ragged, multihued parlance of any sticky retrograde antipodean public house, you wouldn't piss up somebody's arse if their lower colon was on fire, would you? Your parents must have really made a fuss of you, furnishing your pubescent bedroom with pony posters, meccano sets and twee little trophies. Huh! Return at once to the patented Helen's Never Fail Five Point Am I A Needy Fuckwit Test and remain eternally grateful to anyone who dares touch the evil penumbra of your all-encompassing selfishness. One point. And you only received that because you ardently spurn herbal remedies. Go and perform voluntary duties at the terminal ward in a children's hospital, you spoiled naif.

Mostly Bs: Hmmm. You're a little bit giving and a little bit rock and roll. You advance toward any potentially fractious scenario with the ebullient, chivalric ease of an errant medieval knight on Ecstasy. Your marriage of reason with compassion is enviable. Your manners, while far from punctilious, are flawless. You judiciously use your charm, integrity and infinite calm to democratically govern the displeasure of others. My, are you a rare and delicious character. Is there nothing, within reason, that you won't do for the wholesome love and attention of a good man or woman? Two million points, you splendid and rational carer. And a shiny new luxury European sports car. Subtract the ubholstery, the satellite navigation device, the multi-CD player, the unlimited warranty, the ergonomic headrests and one point ninety-nine million points because you cheated outrageously.

Altruistic, perfectly balanced people like you only exist on Aaron Spelling hypernaturalistic television dramas. And they're generally one of the old blighter's own nouveau riche brood.

Mostly Cs: Well, bugger me. You really redefine dire sycophancy, don't you? Your greatest pleasure is abject suffering. Your raison d'etre is to fuel the avaricious happiness of porcine others. Were you, perchance, raised in the stultifying environs of the Catholic Church? If another's moderate contentment is contingent upon your absolute sacrifice, you are delirious with glee and eager to sever any of your offending bodily parts. Your entire life's journey is shaped by the need for forgiveness. With a harsh word, a boot in the face or an elegantly untoward demand you are shriven and delivered to paradise. You are certain that, in essence, your character is wrought from primordial, minacious and original sin. Each punishment you receive and each selfless Herculean manoeuvre you make away from this imagined state of nature is construed by you as a delicious reward. When are you ever going to learn, you sicko? Nobody respects you, people are giggling behind your shirking back, you'll never get your stereo back and if He hadn't been conceptually slaughtered already, God would spurn your company as a minion in Heaven for His omniscient and quite reasonable fear of eternal boredom. Can I get You anything, Your Fluffy Omnipotence? A cup of tea, universal peace or a concentrated protein creme treatment for Your beard? Even our Maker would get the shits. For the sake of a humanity that aspires to one day rashly examine itself and be modestly pleased by its own prognosis, please start telling bossy people who want to have bad sex with you to Just Fuck Off. No points. You are a meddlesome overweening dickhead.

Now, kids, go forth, prosper and enjoy sober, sedentary and safe relationships IF you must have them at all.

CHAPTER TEN

THE HORROR OF GREGARIOUS PEOPLE AND SEVERAL PROVEN METHODS OF HIDING FROM THEM

It has been established from the outset of this text that people are generally vile and stinking. We have also argued that this effluvial stench emanates not from some solid, anterior and immutable fictitious human essence. Human 'essence', as we have learnt, has no scent at all. All social endeavour is necessarily contrived. We are merely artifice. As it happens, that synthesis has soured and its rank and reeking ripeness has hypertrophied to the point where the average nose simply falls off in disgust. Soon, as foretold, we will all be reconstructed. After that, of course, there will be no more wan and perfunctory sex, toxic hospitality or *Hey! Hey! It's Saturday*. Ossie Ostrich will emerge as the unbound crimson id and Red Symons will function merely as fuel to feed the ravenous flaming pyre that signifies a better, stronger tomorrow. Until this glorious day, when ulcerous homophobes are transformed from inexpiable flesh to productive kindling for the celebratory beacon, we must struggle sadly on. We must bear the belligerent bonhomie of the walloping hordes. For not only are they unblessed, iniquitous and putrid but they are FRIENDLY. They want to hang out on your couch.

For many years (she began, wickedly usurping for the nth time the deceptively personable and experiential idiom of billion-selling self-help blockbusters) I laboured under the misconception that my person had the conceptual framework of a tired old sock. Or something like that, in any case. (Analogy has never been my strong suit. This is possibly a decent thing as, so some have posited, the weight of analogy deadens difference. It is a crypto-fascistic linguistic imposition that threatens to deny specificity. Analogy forces different articles and instances to accrue identical definitions. One becomes the pale, inferior and mirrored priv-ation of the other. Again, the toxic power of a dichotomous belief system rises to stifle all! I am positive that Roland Barthes would have agreed with me that analogies are intrinsically evil. That is, of course, had he not been unconditionally squashed by a Parisian laundry truck in an instant of pure existential cruelty. Have I mentioned that?) Whatever. A sock, a stocking or some flimsy encasement are items with which I chose to compare my explor-able, floppy shape. I was responsive only to the presence of people. I needed to cordially consume accursed amigos in order to fill my persuadable tunic. My pliant soul was a velveteen ashram craving the comfort and purposeful thrust of chummy society. My zest took only the form of those who informed it. Aaah, the baleful and binding pellicle of relentless conviviality! This cheery caul eventually began to make me itch and long for pure hypo-allergenic solitude. I realised with a start that nobody seemed to like anyone else terribly well. As a (dismally average) university student, I was proud that my address book was full. I was smug in the knowledge that not a single evening passed without my attendance at some poisonously jovial fandango. I nestled deep in the furrows of fatuity confident that I could call at least fifty people My Dear Friend. Oh, how fucking fascinating I was. I performed the usual first year ritual of returning to darkest suburbia with barely factual narratives chronicling the urban contradistinguished clever stunts of my many many many delicate new friends. Oh, yes! Some of them were even from OTHER COUNTRIES. (I am horribly embarrassed by this latter boast now. If I could not, indeed, count non-Anglo Celtics amongst those of my immediate acquaintance, then I would surely be a racist, antique prude from Ipswich.) Rather judiciously, my mother told me to shut the fuck up and to stop being so conspicuously middlebrow. In any case, I loved my collegiate chums!! As a (dismally average) drop-out, I recounted the experiences of my undergrad companionship. Wasn't everybody indiscriminately sleeping with everybody else's squeeze? Didn't I observe chemically altered Rugger Buggers unsteadily produce their penises to urinate on their team captain's CD collection? Weren't vigilant gossips whispering as soon as their purported chums vacated the main quad? She's a bulimic and she's gone off to eat seven hamburgers, purge in the women's refectory loo, reapply her altogether TOO extravagant maquillage and return as if nothing was wrong! Neurotic slut. And so, in capacious terror, I resolved to abjure all needless and unwholesome contacts and I began to bravely endure an emotionally immaculate, albeit relatively friendless and rather solitary, portable new life. Was I really nourished by the caprice of young ladies who openly embraced me yet, once my poorly shod back was revolved, candidly reviled my illogical mode of dress? (Well, I thought it was brave and poignant and resonantly feminist to wear my bra on the outside. Madonna did it, perhaps with a little more flair, and nobody laughed at her!) Was I legitimately nurtured by the nubile gents who fitfully discussed mining policy with me at young socialist shivoos and then once the camaraderie had ceased, the prevaricating little insects, would roguishly postulate that my vagina was not, in fact, of the average female human dimensions? No, came the resounding reply from my incorruptible conscience. I definitely did not need this. I renounced all party spirit and became a mysterious anchoress. I considered isolation in a deconsecrated convent and pondered breeding a bevy of mongrel feline familiars, growing odd, poisonous herbs and chasing away small children with a tubby toxin-secreting larch stick. The only obstruction to my ideal of desolate self-sufficiency was the very real possibility that some hippies would get word that there was a maverick woman ascetic living in an abandoned church and then they'd come to visit and pay homage to my hermetic vastitude and generally give me the shits with all their humming and mindless earth worship. If there's one thing I hate more than a spoiled, peachy and nuggety-bosomed tertiary princess or a WASP Ra Ra Bachelor Of Economics candidate, it's a fucking hippie.

Of course, one requires one or two worthy confidants, I suppose. It is always better to evince misanthropy with a chum no matter how impossibly contradictory such a practice may prove. The Crankiness Template does have multiplayer and interactive application capabilities. In this case, the sort of snug alliance to reach for is that defined by Patsy and Edina: allies in disdain, interdependent and mutually reliant upon the other's unblinking and identical bitchiness. The only pure, true and reliable friendship is that which provides ballast for your vehement critique of the world. You should not aspire, as previously advised, for fernickity complementarity. You should not seek to absorb and marshal your peers' enthralling difference. You should strive, however, to be unified in your hatred of all objectionable things and to be most especially (and, quite possibly, needless to state) equally inimical to the endomorphic stupidity of Daryl Somers. Sadly, but intriguingly, men cannot lay claim to cartoonish role models so absolutely fabulous as Patsy Sloan and Edina Monsoon. These hapless needy gents must enact a vigorous spot of gender reassembly (see relevant chapter) so that they may begin to share in such an enduring, perverse and wonderfully incorrigible union. Sadly, gents' capacity for wicked friendship has been tainted by the obtuse musculature of Buddy lore. Do you honestly think that Peter Fonda and Dennis Hopper have nearly as much fun as the women of Holland Park? Certainly, their drugs aren't nearly as good. Mr Fonda may look rather tasty and immodestly fetching in those revealing leathers and that curiously patriotic brilliant motorcycle helmet but, really, does he ever kick back with Dennis and Jack to discuss anything more frothy and amusing than the deterioration of The American Dream, unjust drug legislation and the availability of disease-free prostitutes within the city limits of New Orleans? As for Keanu Reeves and River Phoenix in Gus Van Wank's execrable and fuzzy let's-refrain-from-enforcing-the-hypocritical-moral-standards-of-a-placid-whitebread-middle-America-and-while-we're-at-it-let's-refrain-from-enforcing-the-standards-of-a-bearable-motion-picture, *My Own Private Idaho*, urgh. No time for a boyish lark, jolly hockey sticks and good old comradely brouhaha here. All that irritating Shakespearian babble, those unbecoming and muddied suede jackets and abysmal guitar playing. Where is the love in that, I demand to know. Intense masculine friendships appear to offer very little in the way of amusement, genuine leisure or levity.

This is not, of course, to infer, even for a millisecond, that women's friendships are all idyll, unproblematic candour and shopping. As I must remind myself frequently and regretfully,

Patsy and Edina are not actual people. In fact, I have heard that Jennifer Saunders is happily married to Ade Edmondson from *The Young Ones* and is respected as rather a worthy type. Frighteningly, Joanna Lumley is a macrobiotic eater, happily alcohol free and regularly attends the gym. Well, you don't maintain those majestic cheekbones, perky bosoms and enviable Tracii Lords-type pins well into your middle era for nothing, I suppose. Patsy and Edina's nasty friendship is nought but a delicious hyperbolic myth. The unprepossessing truth often is: women can prove to be tiresome companions.

While men speak with each other gruffly, sparsely and with self-conscious profundity, pausing only in their spare conversation to occasionally and surreptitiously urinate on one another's vehicles, women chat pleasantly, volubly and with self-conscious caprice, pausing only in their overabundant exchange to occasionally and surreptitiously urinate on one another's egos. An inordinately malnourished sister of mine used to prettily intone, 'Oh, Helen, you're so LUCKY to be SO voluptuous and ample' which translates roughly as 'Hey, chubby, haven't you got the feminine integrity to subsist on a maximum daily intake of seven mung bean shoots, a crowd pleaser tub of Ford Pills and one child's portion of dolphin-safe tuna sashimi?' (I assume that I am not the first to note the hypocrisy endemic to the 'dolphin friendly' marketing of fish produce. What about the poor fucking tuna? Not a thought is spared for the hapless common ichthyoid, merely because he or she is unable to balance balls on a mammalian snout, perform covert experiments on humans and, Tom Cruise-like, sycophantically rescue profligate divers from shark attack. Is there no justice nor imperishability of will to be discerned anywhere in this gruesome world?) Twisted, retrograde Nietzschean, overcoming, will to power, fascist mullet. At least

I've got tits. The other monstrous fault of women friends, when they are not wowing you with their abdominal tone, banging on about how they can eat and eat and eat and never gain a microgram and generally recounting their currency within the heterosexual economy, can be their ability to metamorphose when a gentleman appears. This has been well documented both in text and in common conversation and hardly bears restating. Suffice to impart, however, that one morally enfeebled crone of my acquaintance could be chatting ably about the convoluted plight of post-Soviet feminists in an unchecked capitalist and Other Objectifying free market and then immediately replicate a *Girlfriend* magazine ethos, annihilate her palpable IQ and show at least three centimetres more cleavage the very instant any unsuspecting male appeared. But, Goddess, I am tiring even myself in recording these poorly disguised homilies and so, poor bruised reader, my sympathy is all yours.

I conjecture that we have all, regardless of gender specificity, incurred the peculiarly flavoured shame of betrayal by a friend. It is perhaps more prodigiously embarrassing to bear this companionate distress than it is to muddle pridefully through the pain of a shattered intimate relationship. When one is dumped by a tempestuous bunny-bear, one can always easily borrow an expedient, immediately plausible and axiomatic explanation from the ratified lonely hearts procedural code. She Wanted To Grow. He Didn't Give Me Enough Space. It Wasn't Her, It Was Me. We Wanted Different Things. She Slept With My Sister. His Thesis Was Blocking The Entrance To My Vagina. This type of orthodox excuse neatly precludes the possibility of further explanation. However, there is no such technology available to the recently friendless who wish to thwart a nefarious emotional intrusion by creeping inquisitive others. Furthermore, we seem unable to deal with the demise of a friendship ourselves, much less to competently relay the details of destruction to another. Why did a certain young lady (who shall remain anonymous just in case she ever buys plants at my mum's shop), with much portentous augury, leave me stranded, punctured and bemused on the asphalt in year eight? Was it because I refused to grow bosoms with her adipose alacrity? Was it because I favoured green garbedine slacks teamed with a yellow rollneck skivvy while she, flaunting institutional convention and wildly embracing the style of the year nine cool group who sat on the cricket pitch at recess (much, I am sure, to the chagrin of first grade cricketer Michael Bevan who apparently attended my high school) suddenly began to dress in a hot magenta, lasciviously polka-dotted, snug minidress? Was it because she adored the *Footloose* soundtrack while I had begun to listen to public radio and favoured the British New Wave? I didn't understand her motives back then and the logic of her ceremonious dismissal of me remains elusive. She simply stated, 'I've talked about it with my mum and she agrees, it's not good for us to be friends. I'm going to sit over there with the cool group now. Don't even think about following me.' And that was it. Three years of close, academically competitive conviviality that spanned two scholarly institutions trashed in the first half of little lunch. Anyway, at the apex of our association I confided in her that I was going to grow up and write books while she murmured something about wanting to be a marine biologist (Why do so many kids want to fiddle about with plankton?). So, nyah. I grew up and wrote books (not exactly my plan of Conrad meets Burchill in a wistfully telluric yet stochastically urban quasi-literary postmodern irrevent framework, but they're still books) and she went on to an apprenticeship in a suburban hairdresser. So, nyah. If she'd hung out with Helen a little longer, she'd probably be cleaning out Orca's blow-hole at this very instant. (I hasten to add that there is nothing that I consider to be remotely wrong or inferior in the acquisition of gainful employment at a suburban hair salon. I once received an unparalleled and inimitable haircut at the hands of an adept technician in a salon at Bexley North. So please remain charitable and forgive this unintentional implication on two counts: there is a capacious conceptual chasm between the desire to meddle with fish and the will to enhance blonde tips. Patently she did not achieve her objective, sciolistic little minx; and obviously, I'm still very pissed off.)

Such hapless scenarios are common, or so I tell myself to assuage the teeming agony. No really. Just about every honest person I know admits to having been scurrilously, overtly and nonsensically discharged of their duties as amiable consort. In adulthood, the defacement of friendship by some unwilling and erratic quoit tends to be a little more arcane. Rather than employing confessional, indiscreet and leaky schoolyard tactics as in, 'I have found a new friend with an in-ground swimming pool. You and your Clark Rubber shit can just go and get fucked now, please'; adults will hint at 'The End' more abstrusely. Grown-ups will becloud, curtain and effectively secrete their disapproval. They will enigmatically veil their discontent and adumbrate thus, 'Oh no, I'm *sorry* I can't come to your wine and cheese evening because ... well, I've just found out I'm lactose intolerant.' As we all know, an aversion to dairy products should prove no immovable obstacle to a long and delightfully perplexing association. So you insist you'll buy some of that curdled soy bacteria masquerading as cheese and a bottle of that repugnant organic merlot. 'Well,' they begin cryptically, 'It's just that I have my um ... Ninjitsu lesson on that night.' You offer to bring along one of your shinto mates, move the potlatch to another month, have the house holistically fumigated and negative ion generated and provide a door to door limousine shuttle service. After much befogging and chic effacement by your wretched soon-to-be-erstwhile plonker friend, you lose your temper and demand substantial marginal gloss. They are then impelled to nakedly admit, 'Well, it's just that I can't fucking stand you. And neither can Susan. As for that gaudy, blowsy wife of yours, well she's always used way too much saturated fat in her preposterous culinary delinquencies and the state of your arteries throughly sickens us both.' As one whose past is aswarm with an army of neglected, affronted or ungrateful companions, please accept my assurance that your life will be monumentally easier to marshal without the bother of the fastidious Susan and her irksome husband.

Not only is the reticence of the adult abhorrent compared to the revelatory candour of a hedonistic pubescent (see Chapter Six, Naughtiness With Impunity, my austere, august and oft-quoted guide to the acquisition of Protracted Adolescence Disorder) but it must be noted, before our immersion in the rigours of this fragment's Never Fail Five Point Plan, that youngsters prove more worthy than their parents in selecting a firm impetus for ruining a friendship. It is infinitely more pardonable, I postulate, to dispose of an unwanted companion because they do not possess an in-ground, tastefully landscaped and prettily embel-lished solar-heated lap pool than it is to consign a former consort to humanity's feculent landfill dump because they are 'spiritually impoverished'. I have observed bizarre putative adults further impede their altogether friable belief systems with New Age grandiosity and then immediately deport their 'unenlightened' friends from their neo-mystic pastel province. As previously established, no-one loves a hippie anyway, so they're simply performing a necessary service. Nonethless, the adult's capacity for maggot never ceases to repulse me. (NB: Do not misinterpret me. I was merely referring to the capriciousness of utter idiots and not to the informed and sterling harsh judgments of the phrenically abled. If, for example, you discover that your most treasured amigo along with whom you grew, lost and loved is a Liberal voter—particularly the sort who occasionally gives their preference to the Democrats in the Upper House, who obsessively attends WWW communal wine tastings and who passionately cares about the sanctity of The Environment while not giving a fuck about native title, a social safety net, subsidised child care or anything else that is decent and worthy and wholesome and which the sale of Telstra may not actually pay for—you are justified, nay compelled, to shoo them instantly.)

Having rabbited fuzzily and cheerily for some rodentate time, our unsentimental action encroaches! We have encountered the truth that friendships are troublingly involute and frequently painful and unrewarding arrangements. We have duly noted the Patsy and Edina model of neo-Platonic love and we have confronted our failure to duplicate their embossed platinum card perfection. We have determined to vigorously springclean our forlornly dusty attachments and we prepare for the onset of our skulking, solitary hibernation.

HELEN'S NEVER FAIL FIVE POINT PLAN FOR OUTRUNNING ROGUES, ROUTS AND REVELS

1.

Orate. No single process quite so expediently repels the attention of bothersome others like the habit of cadenced orotundity. As previously discussed, heroid, polysemous and prudent speech really gives most people the shits. A lavishly delivered sermon by you will send them screaming messily out the door never to return nor, most likely, to invoke your name except to gasp, 'Fuck, stay away from that Helen girl. She's weird.' Your propitious, beautifully structured magniloquence will not only terrify undesirable turds by the complex notions its own fluid unravelling craftily liberates and synthesises. Your sonorous self-consciously significant and sensible spruiking will also effectively shame their twee, vulgar, squeamish rhetoric by extreme contrast. Your slick recital will crush both their desire to remain within a five kilometre radius of you and the frail conceptual core of their boorish blandishments. Well done! All you really need to repulse most stupid fucking idiots is a sentence employing a word such as 'elegiac', 'unprincipled' or 'gelato' and they'll scamper as though they were engaged in the Dance Of The Flaming Arseholes. (Please refer to Helen's Never Fail Five Point Plan For Ladies Who Wish To Enact Extreme Gender Travesty, article 2, 'nudify', in Chapter 7, for a more thorough explanation of this primarily male enacted urban Australian ritual.) Always remember, most poor sods are informed almost exclusively by the linguistic might of *Hey! Hey! It's Saturday*, so they're bound to be suspicious of anything remotely 'foreign'. (Such a reaction was momentously embodied by the Stupid Fuckwits' elected federal representative Pauline Hanson in an 'uncompromising' *Sixty Minutes* interview profile. 'Are you xenophobic?' demanded the Channel Nine stalwart, who had, no doubt, recently completed the MTV Book Club's condensed Brett Easton Ellis volume of the month. 'Please explain,' came the imperative reply. Pauline Hanson is so thuddingly thick and xenophobic that she even fears the verbal expression of a concept that gestures toward her condition. She is not only afraid of 'foreign' things but she is afraid of words that depict this fear. She is xenophobic of xenophobia. She probably even finds the simultaneous practice of breathing and chewing gum to be insurmountable. How she manages to match her pearlised nail varnish and handbag is quite beyond me.) As advised earlier, I recommend the purchase of a decent dictionary, a good thesaurus (not one that is simply alphabetised, they're far too deadening) and a basic encyclopedia of etymology. This should assist you in shedding your most undesirable companions in a trice.

2
Succeed. As my unpopular and damaging attendance at the recent punctilious wedding ceremony and reception of a high school chum will attest, even the most modest professional or personal triumph will disperse your peers. As the tired adage postulates, success is indeed an effective revenge. Admittedly, my life's vanquishments are even rather than inordinate. However, that did not stop me from borrowing a Prada frock, fibbing wantonly about my credit rating and contriving outrageous narratives concerning my involvement with key Labor party powerbrokers to share with all. My flashy deceit procured the desired effect. By evening's end, a young lady (who shall remain anonymous, just in case she still shops at my mother's fine nursery where you will receive a handsome 10% discount on all mountable staghorns, succulents and selected hydrophilic accoutrements with proof of purchase of her daughter's excellent book) had begun beating me as mercilessly in the prettily furnished restaurant ladies rest room as she had some ten years earlier in the considerably less salubrious and perfumey surrounds of the Weston Creek High School girls' loo. With each deft and girlish blow to the head, I felt shriven. The sins of my high school insipidity were washed

away by the violent baptism performed by this nuggety miss as she doused my blonde head in impure bidet water. Despite my bedraggled do, a previously flawless maquillage savaged by nails and made motley with bruises and a mangled, distressed and bloodied designer frock, I exited victorious as the gathered coven incredulously indicated my altogether too tasty consort and exclaimed, 'But I always thought she'd grow up to be a lonely dyke!' Such is the pleasure of real or imagined success. Needless to impart, my presence is no longer sought at such tiresome functions. My one regret was the absence of a certain cocksure suburban hair stylist who had left me stranded on the asphalt in year eight during the first half of little lunch. Please learn by my example. At competitive reunions, exercise a little more urbane caution than the sweetly artless and artificially flaxen Romy and Michele and you shall be rewarded by your future exclusion. Beg for the loan of a sleek outfit, research your lies carefully and, if necessary, engage the services of a highly recommended prostitute. Your modest investment will reap handsome rewards in time. Never again will anyone deign to provoke your attendance to trifling bacchanals. Further, you will no longer be expected to purchase incommodious, meagre and pitiful items of celebratory clothing nor importunate Retro-design chrome toasters, imploratory hardwood chopping boards nor beseeching fancy cocktail shakers as gifts for ungrateful shits who never bother to send a gilt-edged thank you card anyway. (Yes. I think the culpable party will recognise themselves here. Huon pine kitchen implements don't come cheap, you know.) Succeed at all costs! Not only will you be despised and assiduously avoided but you will be envied. One could, in attempting to resolutely spurn the company of ravenous others, simply masturbate effusively astride the multi-tiered wedding cake screaming, 'Oh But I Am The Zoroastra of

Legend! Watch Me Transform From Mere Man Into God. I Shall Laugh Abundantly As The Ravens Pick At My Chicane Cadaver!' However, I assert, it is better to be despised than merely pitied.

3

Move. Never underestimate the simple power that changing your street address, email domain and telephone number can afford. You can effectively determine, for a time at least, the precise quality and number of select persons that are furnished with your exact contact details. There is no better security from unabashed and reckless fuckwits than complete address encryption. Tell your service provider that you do not wish to be listed. Inform Telstra that you seek a silent number. Gingerly change your name by deed poll before you register on the local electoral roll. Alleged 'friends' will be simply unable to recover their attachment to you for some weeks. Moreover, they will be precipitously insulted that you did not immediately inform them of your altered designation and, as such, once they have eventually and unadvisedly wrestled you to the ground by means of overbold guilt, they will, more than likely, rashly vow to avoid you for some time. Tremendous. In making your decision to move, prudently consider your proximity to those of your reluctant acquaintance. Are you likely to bump into them in the frozen dessert aisle at Coles? Does that cosily derelict tavern (temptingly replete with taciturn old blokes with countenances the colour and texture of Christmas pudding, a jukebox that wanly blares nothing but 'American Trilogy', 'Evie' Parts One, Two and Three or Tammy Wynette's D.I.V.O.R.C.E. and Pub Tab facilities) bear the risk of invasion by a gormless workmate? Will that musty cornucopia of an ex-libris bookstore attract that idiot you hooked up with in first year sociology whom you have not yet managed to effectively bilk? These are important questions that must be addressed. Sternly regard your priorities. Is the swish bustle of milky cafe society something you really need in your life? Do you have to be so intimate with tawdry and expensive nightclubs? Are outlandishly costly boutiques so vital to you? All such emporiums merely attract loud swinish oinks. I know you may have been, for some fraught time, relentless in your quest to exceed the smug and reputedly retardative confines of suburbia, but THINK, goddamn it. So you've got to take a bus to secure your preferred brand of tossy olive oil. Big deal. You'll be content in your fortressed satellite and out of the reach of sleek little city dwellers. Stay away from chic high-density inner-urban housing conurbations. They only breed violence, crime and conversation. Moreover, your execrably hip friends will think that you are so unfashionable for moving to Toongabbie, East Doncaster or Logan City that they'll never speak to you again. If they do brave a visit to your hidden domicile, cover your tastefully matte cedar floorboards with cheap fluffy rugs, tack pictures of the type that depict blonde women in tennis outfits scratching their unclad bottoms and serve Boston buns, cheese and gherkin finger sandwiches and meat-slaw at a hyperdoilied morning tea. Of course, once news spreads, as it tends to do quite feverishly in the Burbs, of your spotless hospitality, equally irksome yet more pedestrian dotards may seek an audience with you. At this point, use as many abstruse French and Latin phrases as possible, put Big Black's *The Power Of Independent Trucking* on the stereo and serve only those foods which have been sundried, imported or that bear uncommon and non-Anglo names. Preferably all three. Well done. Nobody likes you.

4

Write. Nobody likes the author of parlous text as I am sure Roland Barthes would have conceded had he not been unconditionally squashed by a Parisian laundry truck in an instant of pure existential cruelty. Once, in my misguided convivial past, I had the misfortune to engage in farcical and uninspired sex acts with a fleshless gent who considered himself A Writer. (You may or may not share in my exquisite joy as I am able to report that after a decade of tireless literary struggle he has published little more than skateboard road test reviews and jaded pop-cultural nonsenses that liberally employ the terms 'way rad', 'going sick' and 'filth' in florid periodicals with a pass-on readership of less than twenty thousand.) This emaciated prig (who, I am compelled by forces beyond my control to impart, had no arse to speak of, putrid bong breath and a menagerie of unflattering tattoos … What WAS I thinking?) was in the habit of Conspicuous Writing. When conversation in his mean, ugly, videocassette infested pit of a front room somehow eluded his mastery and veered to a juncture that did not embrace HIM as the primary object of inquiry, he would pad off, poignantly returning with a significant flourish of his (oh so modishly battered) PC lap-top and he would begin to Write furtively at his makeshift escritoire (generally the pizza padded gut of a comatose stoner deadhead flatmate). He, of course, was thoroughly disingenuous. I am sure that he was simply playing blunted-level Tetris rather than challenging Martin Amis' legitimate claim to the crown of Unctuous And Incorrigibly Boyish But Oh So Fucking Clever Literary Blade. His goal, needless to impart, was to beguile all with his irrepressible yen to create. However, the fascinating corollary of this pretentious and repeated practice was that he simply stopped getting invitations to cool parties. Ha. Immediately my hope-gland began to hum with the possibility that I too may be so reviled. After all, I quite liked the idea of doing something that earned you a bit of cash while remaining at home. Further, I'd always got decent marks in lit and, importantly, I could drink at least half as much as my delightful and stylish publisher and still remain upright. So why not Write and thereby effectively disperse many potential friends, suitors and entreaties to partay? For myself, I could never quite credibly attack the prospect of ostentatiously gesturing towards my trusty Mac and pronouncing my Intention To Write in a public place. Although, if you are that audacious I do suggest you attempt this particular path to solitude. It is a local and immediate expedient. The formal published route does, however, have the advantage of warning thousands of potential comrades that it would be in their best interest to stay resolutely away. There is, I am informed, a small and disturbed number of literary groupies to be wary of. Between magnums of South Australian shiraz, the aforementioned delightful and stylish publisher often assures me that these folk are feeble, easily frightened and generally under the sedated care of an accredited mental health professional. On the whole, it appears, the public perception of authors is that they are unprepossessing, ungainly psycho hose-beasts to be cautiously avoided. One may be passionate, for example, about the purposefully postmodern prose of Jeanette Winterson's later texts. One would also, possibly, be scornful at the prospect of spending an afternoon in her reputedly fiery company. As predicted by some thinkers, the author has become severed from the text. No longer do we valorise writers as the textual truth to be eagerly unravelled and fondly met. Authors, increasingly, bear little relation to the texts which bear their name. In an age where the author is ailing as both a desirable and a public figure, it is circumspect to become one. The author has been killed, as I am sure Roland Barthes would excitedly agree had he not been unconditionally squashed by a Parisian laundry truck in an instant of pure existential cruelty. No one's going to bother a dead guy.

5

Elude. Although, as mentioned in the chapter chronicling the nature of Intimate Relationships And How To Avoid Them, the billion selling feminine-demonic treatise *The Rules* suggests employing mystery as an essential tool in achieving entanglement, I propose that emerging at your next engagement as an impassive, confusing Creature Unlike Any Other will work to really shit people and so secure your wholesome solitude. We all, I conjecture, have endured the rare company of that fugitive relative who is hazy, equivicatory and quietly haughty. You can recognise the miscreant by his or her pained oral emissions. I have a clansperson (who shall remain anonymous in case she/he may one day choose to avail her/himself of the amusing garden statuettes, novelty sprinklers, invaluable horticultural assistance, intriguing autoirrigation devices, terraced water features, durable outdoor furniture ensembles, startlingly effective lawn starters, verdure-ensuring fertilisers, promising bulbs, fetching deciduous seedlings, pod germinators or any of the sterling varieties of potting mix on offer at my mother's excellent nursery that are all, incidentally, available at a sizable discount of 10% to proven legitimate owners of this volume) who has marshalled the noise 'Mmmmm'. After years of unswerving rehearsal, this malleable sound could ably convey disenchantment, boredom, resignation, obdurateness, remorselessness, lofty pity and, above all, detachment in any combination. In refusing to affix an immutable meaning to this single noise, the kinsperson remained coldly elusive and recondite. As a gregarious youngster I was troubled by the impermeable complexity of this 'Mmmmm' noise and sought to warmly engage its architect. I attempted to resolutely understand the nuances of the evasive utterance and, with the mindless optimistic altruism of the very young, soothe what I imagined to be the torment of its owner. After some years, I acknowledged that the unapproachable author of the 'Mmmmm' simply wished to be left alone. They had been diligently reducing the chance, year by year, of receiving invitations to christenings, birthdays and rambunctious noels. The Mmmmm-ster had effectively achieved isolation after years of evincing polymorphous profundity. My confusion and reluctance to buy this person Christmas gifts of any value soon turned to a begrudging respect. Although I quite adore my immediate family, I wondered that I had not devised a similar verbal prophylactic for myself to use in appropriate circumstances. I suggest the immediate acquisition of such a deadly implement. My speech seems to have evolved an exclamation similar to, although a little more unwieldy than, the 'Mmmmm' which I use quite a lot in futile workplace meetings. As an initial form of defence I would murmur, 'That'd be great!' After some months I excised the exclamation. I abbreviated the sentence to a barely discernible, 'Be great.' Presently I am unsure as to whether I should allow the demands of mystique to purloin the 'be' or the 'great'. 'Be' I fear would prove too obfuscatingly meaningful. 'Great', however, is good and bland. It easily invokes disapproval, chagrin and grandiose disinterest in turn. I suggest that you examine the more oft-repeated filaments of your speech and self-consciously build a flexible idiom fortress.

Orate with involute conviction and will. Succeed at any cost and rub it in the noses of your pernicious schoolmates. Move far away and neglect to leave a forwarding address. Write yourself into non-being. Elude everyone regally. Of course none of these tasks are particularly easy to perform. I do wonder that there is such a vast stinking heap of books devoted to the instruction of enhancing one's appeal. It is far more worthy and problematic to effectively alienate annoying shit-heads. Be strong. Remind yourself throughout your Odyssey that there will be no patient and faithful Penelope to mend Poseidon's ravages! You are alone. Trust no-one.

CHAPTER ELEVEN
WHY DO I FUCKING BOTHER?

Actually, I'm rather proud of this particular chapter title. After some months of trying my hand at this messianic self-help palaver, I discern that I am finally able to excrete the sort of warmly rhetorical yet fantastically desperate question that is endemic to bestselling hippie whinge classics with abundant and authentic ease. Why Do I Fucking Bother? It has an eerily complacent resonance, don't you think? I have done rather well and so I ignite the oil burner of decorative self-regard, offer a sacrificial nut roast to the benevolent gods and affirm my ability to formulate twee crap with the dexterity of a Deepak, the homoeostasis of a Hay or the glossolalia of a Gray, Doctor John. Why Do I Fucking Bother? In time, I venture, this deftly devised interrogatory will take its place alongside other honourably bland, falsely heuristic New Age axiomatic challenges such as Why Do I Love Too Much? Why Can I Not Love Enough? When Will The Loving Start? Where Did All The Love Go? or Who Left The Fucking Love Out On The Kitchen Bench AGAIN After I Pleasantly And Patiently Suggested Time And Again That It Should Be Returned

To The Fridge Immediately After Use? In the future, my humble inquiry will be, like those aforementioned, wistfully remembered as the origin of a hitherto unacknowledged late twentieth century discontent. Why Do I Fucking Bother? I am very proud.

Perhaps I exceed myself. How can I make such a vainglorious claim when I hear the very same foul, wet utterance tumble from the lips and besmirch the diffident and dithering chin of at least one disenchanted citizen every single day? I must have unguardedly succumbed to the substandard self-help author's compulsive desire to be fondly remembered as the familiar fuzzy architect of an easily remembered, portable, naked, no-frills resolution. Please excuse my arrogant folly. Conceivably, the only similarity between the question that I have posed and those beseeching, clumsy dissections made by oft-read neo-Mystic demi-thinkers lies in the limited probability of a solvent response to each. Do I Exist? Who Am I? Why Are We Here? Is Righteousness The Same As Piety? Is There Evidence Of God? What Is This Thing For? Why Do I Fucking Bother? The retort to each resounding, ageless investigation is: Well, I Don't Know. Don't Look At Me. Who Am I, Anyway? Mandrake?

Within this fractious text we have messily discussed the relative fatuity, buffoonery and bathos of contemporary ills such as fame, mass communications, gender, intimate relations and 'Platonic' relations. We have briefly examined the daftness of Plato's own giddy dialectic musings, we have gestured toward Aristotle's epagogic lunacy (well, sort of) and we have extravagantly mourned the untimely demise in 1980 of Roland Barthes who, lest it escape your notice, was unconditionally squashed by a Parisian laundry truck in an instant of pure existential cruelty. As attested at the outset of this Manual For A Manageable Misanthropy, I never really finished my degree. So when unpicking the spongy bright sutures that bind puny belief systems, my concentration has been more ably affixed to the accessible unknotting of expungable New Age 'philosophies'. Such ventures have led us only to crushing realisations. We have established that a great deal of that which consists in the world is broke, vile and deleterious to our health. Our vigilant degustation of society's least succulent parts has left us nauseous. We have decried many brisk popular subpsychological solutions to this turmoil. There are numerous problems which defy repair. We have determined, in short, that just about everything is fucked. So, why do we fucking bother?

I have shared in early chapters my belief that in the proximate future all human endeavour will unravel, become wisely molten and fluctuant and then eutectically reassemble to prepare a fertile fluid template for a brighter fleshier tomorrow. There will come a reconstructed time when Channel Nine will offer its battered consumers a televised prime-time commercial-free apologetic textual reappraisal of the now internationally reviled *Hey! Hey! It's Saturday*. This lavish attrition will be hosted by Ossie the Unbound Id and shall feature interpretive dance interludes by the Fitzroy Free and Intuitive Movement Workshop chronicling both the ethical paucity of Daryl Somers and the history of class struggle. The Red Faces panel will include such blunt yet virtuous and steadfast regulars as Julia Kristeva, Angus Young and Fidel Castro. Robert Hughes will have the pleasure of pummelling a human gong whose part will be enacted in turn by Jean Baudrillard, Jeff Koons and the nude, pilose buttocks of a penitent Red Symons. Pluck-A's suit will be filled by a remorseful John Howard and lucky contest winners will receive the random opportunity of driving home in a spanking new oxygen-propelled eco-compunctious Nissan or, perhaps, hearing the contrite duck apologise repeatedly to indigenous Australians while offering equitable and generous compensation packages. No longer a coy counterrevolutionary, Molly Meldrum will re-emerge in a fetching pastel twin-set and tweed skirt sans cowpoke hat to review and ably critique all volumes of Foucault's *History Of Sexuality*. Needless to impart, he'll merely focus on the topic of polysexual liberation and leave the business of contemporary music news to a more competent junior. Finally, having returned from a rewarding and intimate off-shore liaison with a pre-eminent feminist psychoanalytic scholar, Jo-Beth Taylor will powerfully outrun the strictures of Barrel Girldom and return to the site of her former humiliation to eloquently and seductively unravel antique patriarchal thought employing a beef effigy of Jamie Packer and a speculum. All ills will be revised by a sorrowful mass media.

Unhappily, we may have to wait a while for such abashment. For the present, however, our assay looms bleakly. Who should we fucking bother? As a decidedly privileged female citizen who received relatively generous rewards for her trouble, I should be both smug and certain. I am neither. I am skittish when forced to devise reasons for my continued existence. I am without a suitable guide. History's Great Thinkers provide no suitable help. Descartes's cogito has been ably wrestled by agile minds and, from the very little I know, all epistemological efforts have been similarly, brutally and bleakly disqualified. One could turn, I suppose, in desperation to the jerry-rigged contemporary poets of popular culture. Deranged folk such as Michael Bolton appear to offer exuberant and bounteous replies to the plaintive grizzled cogitative pleas of an anxiously vacillating humanity. Generally, balding Mike's answers boldly feature the concept 'You'. 'How Am I Supposed To Live Without You?' The forlorn and intolerable 'I Told You That I Loved You But I Lied'. Implicit in each egregious anthem is the assumption that the presence of an Other will rescue the awkward, mawkish and tonsorially challenged balladeer from an existential crisis. We were, of course, dissuaded from clinging to this pointless belief in the chapter entitled Intimate Relationships And How To Avoid Them. Pensive French pundits can offer no abatement to our woes. Deepak and his amply fragranced mates will bear us no solace. Drugs are but a provisional rejoinder to our screeching demand for a substantial alibi. And Michael Bolton will merely drive the already ambivalent scholar of human endurance to pointless and extreme acts of physical self-assault. What is there to be done?

Oh dear. Do you detect shades of affected nihilism in these, my final words? Is my tone hovering somewhere between Nick Cave's worst lyrical offering and Renton's bleating monologue in the opening sequence of *Trainspotting*? But I am a healthy plump girl with an avowed disdain for needles and public melancholy! I had hoped to overcome. To struggle valiantly from the tepid and impure waters of my own disconsolate salt bath of stinking and grain confusion! It has become sufficiently clear to you by now, dear punctured reader, that I am not Friedrich Nietzsche and that I have neither the bravery nor the wit to exceed myself. I have no answers and nor does anyone of my immediate acquaintance.

I would advise, in closing, that you view your most unbearable travails as a form of exercise. Understand all human exchange as a form of endurance enhancement. I am sure that we all concur that there is no afterlife governing karmic principle. So don't suppose that you are going to be openly rewarded for your notional musculature! Just try to be pleasant and succinct. Avoid eating too many hippies and saturated fats. Maintain a robust sense of justice and, above all, use your noggin and take extreme pride in your advanced citizenship. Don't top yourself and if you do occasionally find your hopes dashed upon the savage rocks of despair, take heart. Depression, after all, is often a manageable device. Get to know the engine of your sadness intimately and take it out for a safe and learned spin where appropriate. Remain inquisitive and enrol to vote.

Perhaps if you can supply an excuse for our continued existence, you might find the time to email me.

In Pursuit of Hygiene
Helen Razer

Like so many mildly neurotic, twenty-something female citizens who never actually got around to finishing their arts degrees (oooh, but we are a largish demographic) I had this misguided lust to articulate my anger. Sadly, somewhere between the conceptual and practical processes, I sort of forgot what I was angry about. Or rather, I became angry at my anger, and shortly thereafter, if I recall correctly, angry at my inability to remember what I was angry about. And, frankly, just damn angry about my inability to buy a fetching frock in size 12.

Imagine what it's like for poor Camille Paglia, who certainly does have the look of a woman in intensive beauty therapy. 'Camille, do you want *Wine With Everything* or *Urban Decay Pigeon*? And while we're at it, have you ever considered how your lurid brand of populist revolution is both reactionary and facile? And can I please have a go at your enormous eyebrow?'

While I am tempted to hold *The First Stone* entirely responsible for rewriting feminism to the point where it became about as unifying and useful to the girl-in-the-street as a wonder bra, I'm not quite that small-minded and brittle. There are lots of other folks to blame as well.

Nothing is sacred in this brilliantly ballistic offering from Triple J star Helen Razer, co-author of the bestselling *Three Beers and a Chinese Meal*.

HG Nelson endorses *Three Beers and a Chinese Meal* by Helen Razer and Mikey Robins:

It was a dream come true when Helen Razer bailed me up in Pinaroo between pig shoots and bellowed, 'HG, can you down tool and pencil a big spit for the front of our book?'

I was more than happy to leave it alone for a couple of minutes and get out the Bic because I have always admired the work of Razer and Robins, albeit from a very careful distance.

Look, if you were stuck in the back of a Zodiac inflatable ducking and diving, trying to avoid the French navy inside the Muraroa atoll, I could think of no better companions to have up the back of the boat trying to get a cup of tea going on the Primus than Mikey and Helen.

If you were in local government and had to think of someone who could open a rebuilt jetty in style and after a cheese and Jatz back up and put on an artistic display that would keep the local press rooted to the spot with their jaws dropping, admiration at the solid fun on display, then look no further than the Two Big Rs from Triple J.

If you were out shooting rabbits in the Simpson Desert, out of petrol, out of ammo and out of water, if you were becalmed in the South China Sea in a leaky tub with the Thai pirates circling, if you were asked to hot-foot it along to a celebrity lingerie fundraiser, I could think of not two more appropriate companions than these authors. Believe me, if you fell out of the boat while barra fishing into a creek chocka-block full of top-end crocs, then these two would be the first in after you with the Swiss Army knife clenched between the teeth.

They wriggle. They don't mind doing the senior muppet

work up close on the table in the skimpy brightly coloured underwear for your enjoyment. They can get a very bright and rowdy High C out of the limpest of flutes. They are lewd. They are not afraid of fruit ... But enough of the big puffs.

As soon as I picked up 'Three Beers' I was blown away. The work has a cheesy, prawn in the sun on the turn, dead fish style and feel about it.

As I opened the cover and caught a stench of the work's aroma, I realised that what had been bagged between the covers of this book were the air biscuits and trouser coughs that had escaped from the collective pants of Razer and Robins. I threw the head back and buried the mouth, nose and eyes in as far as I could go, knowing that I would not come up for air for at least four kilometres and that when I did I would be talking funny.

Make no mistake, this book is a stick of ticking Semtex wedged in a transistor twenty thousand feet above the Pacific and two hours out of Sydney. It's that good, and it deserves a second dip, as once around will leave you simply screaming for more. But enough of the leg up ...

My very good friends, this is a book you can exercise to. And don't be surprised if while reading it you get the urge to dash off by yourself and have a wriggle; especially good for this hand activity are pages 15, 97 and 125.

'Three Beers' has got poke up front and grunt up the back and plenty of room for the hips for those along for the ride.

Finally, the opportunity of contributing a spit at the front of this magnificent piece of Australasian literature does give me the possibility of tidying up the scandal that has dogged my own career for the last four decades.

It's true that Mikey Robins is the product of a brief

dalliance that Helen and I had some years ago. There was nothing crude about it—just two fit Australians on the job knowing what goes where.

We promised each other respect when the sun burst through the bedroom curtains in the morning. I believe we both got it. And for mine, even though many said the kid would stiff at the stum, Mikey has kicked on, proved his knockers wrong and every day makes his mother very proud.

Yes, you are there! Look no further. Save the shoe leather. The fingers have done the walking. Simply savour the action and appreciate that Razer and Robins are the big two of the current brown out of Australian literature.

Three Beers and a Chinese Meal
Random House $19.95